ENTRY PLANNING FOR EQUITY-FOCUSED LEADERS

Empowering Schools and Communities

JENNIFER PERRY CHEATHAM
RODNEY THOMAS
ADAM PARROTT-SHEFFER

HARVARD EDUCATION PRESS
CAMBRIDGE, MA

Paperback ISBN 978-1-68253-765-7

Library of Congress Cataloging-in-Publication Data is on file.

Published by Harvard Education Press,
an imprint of the Harvard Education Publishing Group
Harvard Education Press
8 Story Street
Cambridge, MA 02138

Cover Design: Ciano Design
Cover Image: Orbon Alija/E+ via Getty Images

The typefaces used in this book are Adobe Garamond Pro,
ITC Legacy Sans, and Proxima Nova.

*To those courageous
enough to lead together
for racial justice*

CONTENTS

FOREWORD

The spring of this year marks the thirtieth anniversary of my selection as superintendent of schools in Long Beach, California, our
state's third-largest school system. I was literally vetted for the job
during the 1992 Rodney King riots that had engulfed the urban core
of both Los Angeles and Long Beach with unprecedented loss of life
and destruction of property.

In selecting me, an insider African American area superintendent who had grown up in the community but had attended paro-
chial schools, the Long Beach school board seemed to be saying that
if social chaos and disruption were the order of the day, then I was
the person most likely to work with school staff, parents, community, law enforcement, and others to restore order. There was no time
to focus on the historic nature of my appointment as the first person
of color to head the school system following 110 years of white male
leadership, although the *Los Angeles Times* headline did famously an-
nounce: "Minority Selected to Head Long Beach School District."

Because I had a successful ten-year run in Long Beach that cul-
minated in my winning the McGraw Prize and the district winning
the prestigious Broad Prize for Excellence in Urban Education *without* a written and published entry plan focused on equity, a skeptical
reader picking up this new timely book by Jennifer Perry Cheatham
and her colleagues Rodney Thomas and Adam Parrott-Sheffer might

be tempted to cavalierly say something like: "If he can do it without an entry plan focused on equity, then so can I." In my judgment, nothing could be further from the truth. Long Beach would have gotten better a whole lot sooner if the excellent advice coming from this new contribution to organized and thoughtful approaches to leading with equity front and center had been available back when. And even though my time in Long Beach was challenging, it pales in comparison to what our school leaders are facing today in terms of both the COVID-19 pandemic and the racial reckoning, along with the inevitable backlash associated with the same. It's comforting to know that help is on the way with resources like this one.

Each of the chapters in this incredibly valuable book is designed, in a step-by-step way, to help practitioners understand both themselves and the various contexts in which they will be working as they put equity front and center. While I thoroughly enjoyed each one, I really identified with and relished chapter 3 on "understanding context," because it goes a long way toward explaining my brief and not so stellar tenure as superintendent of schools in San Diego, California, the state's second-largest school system.

In 2005, following my award-winning tenure in Long Beach, I was safely ensconced as a professor of practice at the Rossier School of Education at the University of Southern California, when a search firm reached out asking about my interest in returning to the superintendency via San Diego, about ninety miles south of Long Beach. Again, if this book and its critical guidance had been available back then, I believe that I might have done a much better job as superintendent there.

I mistakenly and cavalierly thought that I knew and understood the context because San Diego was "just another Navy town like Long Beach," as I famously said to the eager search consultant at the time. What I didn't know and understand at the time is that context for a new leader is so much more than the service branch of the military that had been there for years. It's multifaceted, and includes the personal, the organizational, the occupational, and the social. My view of the San Diego context was incredibly shortsighted, and that contributed to my brief tenure there.

For example, I had always worn my ability to get along with teacher unions as a singular badge of honor. What I didn't understand about the San Diego context was that the editorial board of the local newspaper was highly suspicious and deeply skeptical of any new leader giving a priority to getting along with unions. This unwittingly influenced—in a negative way—the initial coverage of my entry. Secondly, as an African American who understood that community in Long Beach, I thought that I would easily understand that same community in San Diego. Again, I was wrong. Where the African American community in Long Beach historically identified with the Democratic party, significant elements of the community in San Diego, especially church pastors, identified with the Republican party and actually welcomed the philanthropy coming from the conservative Walton Foundation, which was interested in disrupting the school system by investing in charter schools that would be run out of empty classrooms on church properties.

In chapter 3, these authors brilliantly use the Baltimore case study of Dr. Sonja Santelises' return as CEO to fully dissect in rich detail what the on-the-ground context should look like as a successful entry plan is framed around equity as a guiding principle, and how a new leader goes about putting that into practice.

This important and practical book also delivers a critical message that sometimes can get obscured in leadership careers, namely, that our approach to entry is crucial and may define the course, trajectory, and success of our time in the job. Given the persistent gaps in opportunity and achievement in our schools and districts, in virtually every context, nothing is more important for today's school leaders than framing entry with equity. Throughout this book, these coauthors consistently deliver on that important promise with rich and concrete examples from the field at all leadership levels.

One of my long-standing assignments in an education policy and governance course I teach is to require students to attend a local school board meeting and prepare a written analysis of what they have observed. Because I had been reading the news stories and watching the television accounts of disruption of school board meetings both in Southern California and across the nation, I decided to go to a local school board meeting recently to see firsthand what is going on—and to get a taste of what I was exposing my students to.

Here in the Coachella Valley of Southern California, there are three school systems—Palm Springs, Desert Sands, and Coachella Valley. I chose to attend the Desert Sands meeting, that community being demographically the most suburban and upscale of the three. During public testimony at the packed board meeting, I was treated to a cornucopia of "culture warrior grievance" as speaker after speaker strode to the podium and accused the superintendent and the board of every possible manner of abusing and harming the K–12 school children under their care. Their list of abuses included supporting vaccine mandates for students and staff, teaching critical race theory, and forcing high school students to watch "CNN in the Classroom." A couple of weeks after that board meeting, the superintendent of the district announced that, with the arrival of his first grandchild coming in the spring, he would be retiring as superintendent. As we all know, the Desert Sands superintendent is joining record numbers of superintendents and principals who are leaving their posts as the third school year of the pandemic unfolds.

We need to replace them with a new cadre of leaders who are not going to shrink from or quietly ignore the equity agenda in order to play it safe as this new kind of politics unfolds, which is yet another reason why this book is so important.

I say this to make clear that equity-minded school leaders are under consistent and brutal attack right now in America, and they are going to need every help, road map, and guide in order to be successful. Cheatham and her colleagues have done a masterful job of delineating, step by step, what is needed by principals, superintendents, and other educational leaders in the critical and important areas of context, trust building, listening with empathy, understanding, changing the narrative, and galvanizing for action. Even more importantly, they've captured the real-time voices of leading superintendents, principals, and others to show the reader that this is not some academic tome with no relation to the extraordinary circumstances unfolding on the ground right now with the outcome uncertain.

It's clear that this new brand of school politics is not going away anytime soon. In fact, recent news reports indicate that several states are moving to make school board elections partisan, moving away from the long-standing practice of nonpartisan local school board elections in the United States. While Tennessee, Arizona, Missouri, and Florida are leading this new change effort, it's important to remember that Republicans now control the state legislatures in thirty-two states, more than at any time in history.

We often refer to those on the frontlines of education today as heroes. This important new book is heroic in that it provides critical guidance to those to whom our country currently owes a tremendous debt of gratitude for courageously leading the effort to create a bright future for youngsters who historically have been underserved in our nation's public schools. We won't be able to do that critical and important work successfully without timely new books like this one. A well-deserved and heartfelt thanks to these courageous authors for putting equity front and center in our nation's public schools.

—Carl A. Cohn,
Professor Emeritus,
Claremont Graduate University

INTRODUCTION

—JENNIFER PERRY CHEATHAM

When I accepted the job as superintendent in Madison, Wisconsin, in February 2013, I knew I was walking into an equity leadership challenge unlike any of the challenges I had faced before. My first few months on the job would either confine or expand my possibilities for success.

On the surface, leading the Madison schools might have seemed less complicated than my prior leadership positions. It was a midsize urban district of approximately twenty-seven thousand students in fifty schools. The student body's reported demographics were diverse—about 10 percent Asian, 20 percent Black, 20 percent Latino, 40 percent White, and 10 percent two or more races—and approximately half qualified for free and reduced lunch. There were no segregated schools in the city, thanks to some voluntary desegregation agreements made years ago, and there were no schools that were severely over- or underresourced. The population of English language learners, at 25 percent, was steadily increasing, as was the district's commitment to bilingual education. Students with disabilities comprised 14 percent of the student body, and the district had a strong reputation for inclusive education. It was home to the University of Wisconsin–Madison's top-ranked School of Education, which trained many of the district's principals and teachers, and located in the state capitol. The city was regularly recognized and listed as one of the best places to live in America.

However, Madison's challenges at the time of my entry were profound and multifaceted, as complex as any I had seen. The Wisconsin legislature had recently passed Act 10, which stripped collective bargaining rights from unions, leaving the teacher corps demoralized and the teacher union combative. The school board had just rejected a charter school proposal that would focus on serving Black youth, leading to diminished trust between the school district and the Black community. To make matters worse, just after my arrival, the Wisconsin Council on Children and Families issued a startling report on racial disparities in the city of Madison and the surrounding Dane County. It exposed gaps in Black-White prosperity across dozens of indicators, worse than the rest of the state and the nation, causing shame and confusion for those who benefited most.[1] Madison's White progressive community had not yet begun to reconcile the mounting evidence that systemic racism made it difficult for people of color, especially Black people, to thrive there. Trust was low, the demand for change pervasive, and the school district sat at the center of it all.

Despite these challenges, all I could see were possibilities, including the prospect of entering the district in a way that would honor the depth and complexity of the problems the school system faced, so many related to race and racism. In the design of my entry, I hoped to listen deeply with my head and heart, produce an honest and compassionate assessment of strengths and challenges, build healthy routines for making meaning and learning together, create momentum, and boost confidence. Most of all, I wanted to galvanize a community for action. As a White woman charged with leading an equity agenda, I also understood that I needed to work together with leaders of color every step of the way. By doing so, we could build a foundation together, from which transformational change might grow.

I share this personal scenario because stories like it exist everywhere, each one unique to the leader and the context, but still variations on a theme. These scenarios do not just demand intentional leadership entry, but leadership entry that is focused on equity from the start. This book was written to help new leaders or leaders in new positions use those first months on the job to build the trust, credibility, and impetus necessary for sustainable change in their organizations and the communities they serve.

In it, we share a framework, not a blueprint, for how to design one's leadership entry tailored to context. We tell our stories and share hard-won lessons from those experiences. We share the stories and reflections of other leaders from a variety of backgrounds and stages of their careers, all equity-focused leaders who have been intentional in their initial leadership moves. Most importantly, we invite our readers to reflect on their own stories and experiences. Our intended audience includes leaders of every race, ethnicity, and gender; top leaders in organizations and mid-level managers; people who work in school districts or adjacent to them; and both novice and experienced leaders. Our audience also includes experienced leaders who are pivoting their strategy or refreshing their leadership at a critical time. And while this book focuses on leaders who serve minoritized youth and families, we believe it will be useful for leaders who lead in every context—urban, suburban, and rural—and in communities that are reflective of every demographic group.[2] This book is for any educational leader who wants to design a personal leadership entry plan that is equity-focused and human-centered.

CHALLENGES AND OPPORTUNITIES

The typical problems—and unintended consequences—associated with leadership entry in education are abundant.[3] New leaders risk glossing over local context and history, which can diminish trust and produce blind spots. They may go too fast or too slow, with little communication or rationale, which can cause frustration and confusion. They can sometimes jump to solutions and strategies too quickly, solving the wrong problems and alienating local practitioners and community members. They may rely on data sources and data analysis processes that reinforce negative stereotypes and oversimplified narratives. Practically speaking, even in the best-case scenarios, the process can leave the leader feeling exhausted only a few months into the job.

In public school systems, leadership entry happens in the spotlight, in a high-stakes political environment, often facing pressure for immediate results. Missteps early on can make it impossible to recover, and missed opportunities to develop shared goals, shared understanding, and collective responsibility for progress can result in the onus falling on the leader's shoulders alone. For women and people of color, the scrutiny is even more intense, and the result is that leaders often leave their positions too soon. Superintendents running the country's largest school districts, for example, stay on the job for about six years on average, hardly enough time to make sustainable change, and that tenure is shorter for female superintendents and for superintendents in high-poverty districts or districts with high percentages of students of color, where stability is most needed and where leaders of color tend to lead.[4] Principal tenure is even more problematic, with an average of four years on the job and fewer for principals working in high-poverty schools.[5] Even nonprofit leaders, especially in high-stress fields, have similarly high turnover rates.[6]

Add in the possibility of navigating a crisis during leadership entry, and it becomes even more precarious. From a budget crisis to a student or faculty death to a natural disaster, crises are inevitable in these jobs. In a crisis, a leader must do the day-to-day work while simultaneously grabbing on to the opportunities the crisis affords. Gianpiero Petriglieri, an expert on leadership and learning, states that leaders must also "hold" the people they serve during crises. He says, "In psychology, the term has specific meaning. It describes the way another person, often an authority figure, contains and interprets what's happening in times of uncertainty."[7] During a crisis, leaders must put their communities at ease through information flow and transparency, provide opportunities for voice and influence, and take care of people, all essential skills for leadership entry.

Today, however, the stakes have never been higher. As a result of the crisis wrought by the COVID-19 pandemic, new education leaders must do more than stabilize their organizations and communities; they must find a better way forward. According to Linda Darling-Hammond from the Learning Policy Institute, "It's clear that COVID-19 has launched us into a new era for education. If we get it wrong, we risk widening opportunity and achievement gaps in ways that will have long-standing impacts on our society and economy. But if we get this right, we may be able to finally achieve the empowering and equitable learning opportunities for all children that will provide the foundation for a thriving future for us all."[8] In other words, new leaders now have an even higher standard to meet, and there is already evidence that leadership turnover has increased as a result, especially in the superintendency.[9]

These challenges are further amplified when we consider that the movement for racial justice in the US demands that institutional leaders everywhere focus on racial equity and other forms of oppression in their organizations from day one—inequities that have been magnified by the current health crisis—no matter their demographics. In education, racial inequity can take countless forms: unequal access to advanced coursework, absence of representation in the curriculum, lack of diversity among the workforce, or disproportionate use of exclusionary disciplinary practices; all of them result in disparate outcomes for Asian, Black, Indigenous, and Latinx youth. Every form reminds us of the reality that "racial groups are not standing on approximately equal footing."[10] Addressing structural and systemic inequities requires moving beyond acknowledging gaps between racial groups, which education leaders have been doing for the past twenty years of education reform. Instead, they need to create deliberate and intentional racial equity strategies from the beginning.[11] Leadership entry, then, must be even more deliberate if the leader is going to identify the root causes of the problems their organizations and communities face, address problems rooted in systemic racism, galvanize a collective effort to face those problems head-on, and stay long enough to see it through.

Altogether, leadership entry in education is daunting, in that it demands leadership through complexity. As complexity experts David Snowden and Mary Boone explain, a "complex" system involves large numbers of interacting elements, a past and present that are intertwined and evolving, and external forces that are continually changing.[12] This reality ought not to paralyze the incoming leader. It merely emphasizes the importance of understanding context and expanding skill sets beyond the typical leadership moves. In other words, leadership entry in a complex environment is not as simple as diagnosing an organization and developing a plan. While best practices and experts and strategic planning processes certainly can get a new leader to a plan of action, leadership entry with attention to complexity requires looking for patterns, fostering ideas from those closest to the problems, and encouraging their growth. As Snowden and Boone suggest, "That is why, instead of attempting to impose a course of action, leaders must patiently allow the path forward to reveal itself. They need to probe first, then sense, and then respond."[13]

We believe the entry of a new leader is an ideal time to begin the process of meaningful, equity-focused change, provided the leader is ready to start strong. That is because beginnings matter. Whether one is a new superintendent or central office leader looking to refresh goals and provide direction, a principal striving to transform a school's culture, or a nonprofit leader who wants to be more attuned to the needs of its clientele or community, what happens earliest in the experience is critical. We know from research outside education that events from early in an experience are what people remember the most. There is a productivity bump during the initial period of one's tenure.[14] While we do not think the term "honeymoon period" reflects the reality of those first months on the job, especially now, leadership entry is ripe with opportunities. It offers a tremendous opportunity to gain insight, trust, and commitment to set the stage for collaborative learning, collective responsibility, and positive change that addresses educational inequality head on.

OUR BEGINNINGS

We wanted to write this book for transitioning leaders in the field because we have learned a lot about leadership entry that we think could prove useful for today's leaders, especially those committed to leading for equity. These lessons trace back to our relationships' beginnings and have only grown in depth and dimension over time. Knowing something about these beginnings, we believe, is essential for understanding our stance on this critical topic. We want to enter this book, just like we would enter a new role or a new community, by sharing with our readers a little about who we are and how we came to know one another.

I have known Rodney Thomas since our time working together in the Chicago Public Schools in 2008. When we first met, he was working in an office that focused on principal support, and I was starting as a chief area officer, or area superintendent, assigned to a set of twenty-five schools on the near South and West Sides of Chicago. Rodney had palpable, positive energy, a creative spark, and a love for life and all its challenges and opportunities. Every time I entered his office on the ninth floor of 125 South Clark, usually on Fridays for our weekly area chief meetings, I heard his voice call out from across the room, "Hey, Jen!" And if I ever stepped outside with Rodney onto the sidewalk, he seemed to know everyone. He was masterful at building relationships, exuding warmth and care. He also had a habit of attracting mentees who looked to him for affirmation and guidance.

Given Rodney's passion for talent development, I went to him early and regularly for advice on principal recruitment, hiring, induction, and support. Most importantly, he seemed to understand and appreciate how I was approaching the job. As a White woman, managing a group of principals for the first time without having been a principal, and in a part of the city with which I wasn't familiar, I was planning my entry with the utmost care, resisting any urge to play expert or savior. I knew I needed to work with the existing area team members to build the school support strategy together, drawing on their in-depth knowledge of our schools. I wanted our principals and teacher leaders to form a vibrant learning community, focused on improving student outcomes, so that we could support one another. Perhaps most important, I wanted to be clear to the communities that we served that while I was an outsider, I would listen, seek understanding, and use every ounce of power I could muster to help them make the changes they wanted for their children. One Friday, while riding on the elevator with Rodney and getting his advice on building my team's capacity, he hinted at his interest in joining it. As a Black man, born in the South, raised in Chicago, and committed to supporting communities that reflected his own identity, he had a vested interest in our success. By the time we stepped off the elevator, I had offered him a job as a specialist focusing on talent. We learned together that building and investing in a team of people with multiple perspectives, including historical perspectives, would be crucial to our success as equity-focused leaders.

We loved working together, and we were perhaps an unlikely duo. While we were both about the same age, we had experienced the world differently. I started my life in a working-class neighborhood on the North Side of Chicago. When we moved to a middle-class White suburb where my parents felt we would have a better life, I saw my opportunities expand. Rodney grew up mostly in a Chicago housing project called Cabrini-Green, where he experienced the impact of structural inequality firsthand. While I was taking the train into the city for my violin lessons on Michigan Avenue during high school, Rodney traveled by bus to the far North Side to get a better education. While I stayed in Chicago and went to DePaul University for college, exploring my identity and privilege for the first time, Rodney went off to Grambling State University, an HBCU where, he says, "I learned to see my people as nothing short of brilliant."

Despite our differences, we both grew up in large families with lots of love and deep relationships, so we liked a busy office filled with laughter and lots happening. For us, work was an extension of family. We both started our careers in teaching with a spirit of activism at the core, committed to lifting our students' voices. We believed in shared leadership and the empowerment required for people to do their best work. We shared a vision of what was possible that centered on children and youth's inherent capability. Moreover, we both stood in the discomfort that the world was not as it should be, something that we saw in our upbringings and faced every day as we traveled from school to school. We learned that attention to personal identity and expression of personal values would need to become a recurring theme in our leadership journeys.

In addition to the methodical and focused support we tried to provide our schools, we also positioned our office to solve problems that schools could not solve independently. We listened hard, dreamed big, tried things, and learned along the way. We heard from our teachers that it was hard to find promotional paths in the system, so we started a grassroots program to create more intentional leadership pipelines for star teachers. We heard that Local School Councils in our highest-poverty schools were often struggling to find good principal candidates, so we put on fun and festive professional recruiting events for council members and promising principals to meet one another.[15] We heard that parents did not understand how to navigate the district structure, so we began holding regular parent forums to get their perspectives on our biggest problems. Together, we created a buzz about working in our area of the city that attracted some of the best staff members and principals around. Most importantly, we were starting to get results in student achievement, which told us that there was something about calculated risk-taking that was a critical ingredient for success. We came to understand that the ways of working we embraced early on mattered and began to positively influence our schools' cultures.

There are distinct memories that bond us, too. I remember sitting in the car with Rodney after a visit to one of our schools, Skinner North, located just behind where Cabrini-Green once was. We sat in the parking lot and watched soberly as one of the remaining towers was smashed with a wrecking ball, making room for the Target store that stands there now. I remember thinking that I could not imagine having the neighborhood where I grew up destroyed before my eyes. There was nothing I could do for him in that moment but to bear witness. I also recall a parent meeting in North Lawndale, a Black community on the West Side of Chicago, where parents and teachers had rallied unexpectedly because they had heard a rumor that a local school was on the district's closing list. Because I was the face of the district, I was the focus of their anger and utter frustration that evening, built up over generations. As much as Rodney wanted to step in, he knew he couldn't. Given my position, and my positionality, it was my responsibility to do better. Together, we learned that these moments of holding one another's humanity, and the humanity of the communities we served, were as important as anything we learned to do as leaders for equity.

Adam Parrott-Sheffer was one of those talented principals we were trying to recruit. He had just graduated from the Harvard Graduate School of Education's principal preparation program and had eager, youthful energy that we admired. Born in the suburbs of Chicago, Adam grew up moving a lot, attending six schools in three states, with each move to a wealthier and Whiter community. His earliest and most consistent experience in these schools was getting in trouble for defending classmates mistreated by other students or teachers. As a result, he spent a significant amount of time in the principal's office. However, a summer job in high school, working as a lifeguard alongside a Chicago public school teacher, influenced his thinking about teaching as a meaningful career, one in which he could get into more trouble on behalf of students who deserved better. After several years as a special educator with a focus on reading, Adam decided it was time to return to the principal's office where he spent so much time in his youth. He recognizes now that his early desires to change the world reveal what he calls "a naive worldview unique to those born into generational wealth, maleness, and Whiteness." He also readily acknowledges there is little in his narrative that would suggest that equity and racial justice in schools would become central to his life's work. However, what Rodney and I saw in Adam was a reflective stance that we did not often see in White male leaders. It revealed an understanding that equity-focused leadership requires a lifetime of internal work.

During Adam's search for his first principalship, he put himself in front of more Local School Councils than we could count, and he was dogged. Nevertheless, his boyish looks, cerebral personality, and race made him an unlikely match for our openings. He ended up landing an excellent principalship at Peterson Elementary, a one thousand–student preK–8 school on the North Side, and they welcomed him with open arms. The school was big and diverse, with a student body that spoke thirty-five languages across seventy nationalities. He was hired as an interim principal, which is a little like a year-long interview, but given that this was his first principalship, he did not mind the arrangement. He felt confident that he was the person for the job. At worst, the temporary status would give him a graceful "out" if it was not right in the end. Of course, Adam went on to be an excellent principal, growing into his role as an equity-focused, strategic, and collaborative leader.

And then, the area office structure in CPS was reorganized by a new CEO, our schools and teams split apart, and I accepted a promotion to the central office to lead several high-profile initiatives aimed at improving teaching and learning, which leads to one final observation about our beginnings. Over those first four years that we knew each other, we had four different CEOs. As eager as we were to help each successive leader, rooting wholeheartedly for their success, none of us recall that they used formal leadership entry plans designed to learn about the school system or the community before making change. As a result, each time we experienced a leadership transition, we found ourselves coaching people through yet another reorganization, processing with our teams the next round of mandates or budget cuts, and trying to stay focused on what mattered most to the people working and learning in our schools. These leadership transitions were hard, and harder than they needed to be.

We hope this glimpse into our relationships' start illuminates some of the critical stances that we take as leaders, ones that we have forged through experience. Equity-focused leadership entry is not just about diagnosing the strengths and weaknesses of an organization and creating a plan of action. It is about creating the trust to make real change. It requires understanding yourself and your context. It requires deep listening, acknowledging historical pain, and creating spaces for healing. It requires motivating people, letting ideas emerge, and developing people's capacity to lead with and without you. Ultimately, we understand that our leadership positions are temporary. Your leadership approach, however, especially those steps you make early on, will leave behind ripples, for better or worse, that you cannot even see.

OUR APPROACH

Each of us went on to pursue other leadership roles—me as a superintendent, Rodney as a central office and nonprofit leader, and Adam as a principal and principal coach—in which we each used a planned leadership entry approach. We all drew on the literature (see appendix A), including Barry Jentz's excellent plan book called *Entry: How to Begin a Leadership Position Successfully*. In it, Jentz suggests a "hit-the-ground-learning" approach with attention to complexity so as to develop an "in-depth, collective understanding" of the organization.[16] We are indebted to him for his guidance.

Those early leadership entry moves, which emphasized transparency, relationship building, and learning, certainly helped us build the trust and credibility necessary to make positive change. It also helped us do hard things, get through difficult times, and struggle, learn, and grow with the communities we served. Looking back, however, we also see the missed opportunities. For example, we wish we would have been more explicit about the root causes of our biggest challenges from the beginning, problems rooted in systemic racism and oppression. In hindsight, we wish we had been more attuned to the way power works, not just for political reasons, but to help redistribute it. We also could have done a better job anticipating the emotional burden of leadership entry, especially for leaders of color, and planned accordingly.

This reflection has led naturally to some questions about the design of leadership entry, the kind of "how might we" questions that are often generated at the beginning of a human-centered design process.[17]

How might we:

- Consider our own racial, ethnic, and gender identities as we design?
- Pay closer attention to local history and regional context?
- Identify and understand the real problems our organizations face, especially problems rooted in systemic racism and oppression?
- Communicate our understanding in a way that creates new and true narratives?

- Engage those who have been negatively impacted in designing possible solutions?
- Attend to the pain and trauma experienced by those within the community and provide opportunities for healing?

The current literature provides practical steps, urges a collaborative inquiry approach, and differentiates a little for roles, but it does not adequately address the nuanced leadership moves necessary for leaders with a range of identity markers, especially women and leaders of color, to start their jobs strong. Our goal is to build on this literature by providing new guidance that is much more explicit about leadership entry for racial equity, introduce a more robust and present-day set of leadership stories to guide our work, and frame an ongoing conversation about the leadership dispositions necessary to lead for equity through complexity while sustaining ourselves and our communities.

HOW TO READ THIS BOOK

We begin with an overview of our new Entry for Equity framework, providing a rationale for each dimension of the framework and how it can be used to enhance the typical steps of an entry process. Each chapter that follows focuses on a single dimension of the framework; we further explain the importance of the dimension by drawing on our review of the literature, our empathy interviews with leaders, and our own experiences. Each chapter also features a leadership entry case example with a focus on that dimension, presenting leaders in a variety of roles, with different identity markers and lived experiences.

While the book is grounded in theory and research, it is practitioner-focused and action-oriented, so in addition to the background and case example, each chapter also includes practical implications, a skill to practice, and a set of reflective questions to help with a leader's own personal planning. These ideas have also been compiled into one comprehensive reflective planning tool that can be found in appendix D. We suggest moving methodically through the book, but our readers may want to focus on a particular chapter. For that reason, the book has also been written so that each chapter can stand alone.

As a reminder, the book does not offer a step-by-step plan, or a guidebook, but a framework for individual planning, because context matters. It will require that leaders take stock, take calculated risks, and chart new paths forward with and for the communities they serve. In her book, *Coaching for Equity*, Elena Aguilar states:

> [S]ocial, political, and economic divisions in the United States, and elsewhere, have become even more glaringly apparent. We see where people can't listen to each other, haven't built the skill and ability to learn from each other, lack empathy for each other, and are failing to achieve their goals and visions for peace. And yet . . . the desire for connection, freedom, and healing is stronger than the desire to hurt, dominate, and oppress . . . I believe the human desire for belonging and healthy community is paramount to all others, although I also recognize that some people's actions have not always aligned to this intention.[18]

Our goal is to help new equity-focused education leaders improve their ability to garner the trust, insight, and impetus to make transformational change in education, which we need now more than ever.

CHAPTER 1

THE ENTRY FOR EQUITY FRAMEWORK

We designed the Entry for Equity framework to guide a nuanced set of actions during the first critical months of a job, unique to each leader's identity, role, and context. Developed based on our own experience, a review of relevant literature (see appendix A), and empathy interviews with a range of leaders who have recently started new jobs (see appendix B), we hope that the framework will offer new ways of thinking about leadership entry that have been missing from our collective leadership repertoires. Accompanied by guidance on the typical phases and steps a leader takes during their leadership entry, and with a focus on the most critical skills needed to execute those steps well, the framework provides a set of concepts to guide the design of an equity-focused leadership entry plan.

Our framework introduces eight dimensions that we believe leaders ought to consider in the design of their leadership entry. Taken together, these dimensions represent a theory of action, an "if . . . then . . ." statement that articulates the relationship between actions and outcomes.[1]

If the leader:

- looks inward to understand their multiple identities as well as outward to understand the social, cultural, and historical context of the community they serve;
- commits to transparency in the process, is explicit about issues related to racism and oppression from the beginning, and actively builds trust along the way;

- centers the voices of those who are most experiencing the problems, listens with empathy to multiple perspectives, and develops a shared understanding of the organization's strengths, challenges, and opportunities;
- uses this shared understanding to tell an honest narrative about the organization that disrupts deficit thinking and racial stereotypes and galvanizes the community for action; and
- provides space for healing, self-care, and the care of others

then the leader is more likely to set in motion an equity-focused change effort that can lead to sustainable change. The eight dimensions described below, each interrelated, are essential for leaders who want to lead for equity from the beginning.

THE ENTRY FOR EQUITY FRAMEWORK

The Entry for Equity framework (figure 1.1) is designed to express the idea of building energy, movement, and power to produce change. In our experience, change is never linear, nor is leadership entry, but more like waves or wind, building momentum over time. Like waves, leadership entry is where small ripples can build over time into a powerful force. The framework also captures that every move we make as leaders should be done with trust building in mind and with care for both the people we serve and ourselves. Here, we provide an overview of each dimension.

Understanding Self and Understanding Context

Leadership entry with an equity focus requires that new leaders take the time to reflect on facets of their identities, with a focus on racial identity, in relation to the community they serve.[2] Reflecting on identity is crucial because our identities can provide strength and insight, but they can also produce blind spots, and assumptions can be dangerous when untested. Without reflection, leaders are more

FIGURE 1.1 Entry for Equity Framework

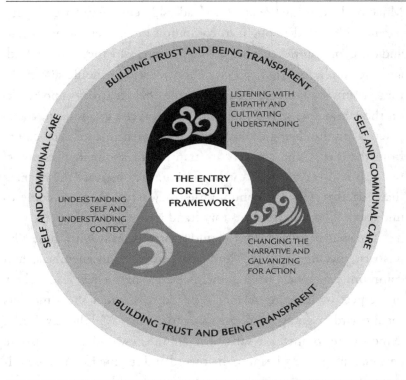

prone to paralyzing emotional triggers as well, common during leadership entry. Looking inward before looking outward is critical, as it will inform early leadership moves.

Equity-focused leadership entry also requires understanding the organizational and community context, including the history of oppression, racial justice leadership, and opportunity.[3] In leadership entry, it is typical for leaders to map the current environment, including its funding, policies, and politics, but it is a misstep to gloss over its social, cultural, and historical roots. A new leader must identify the opportunities to build on success, understand the historical wounds that need healing, and ascertain the possible resistance one might face.

Building Trust and Being Transparent

Much of the existing literature on leadership entry emphasizes transparency. New leaders ought to communicate to their organizations and the communities they serve who they are, why they want to lead, and the core values that will guide them. Leaders should also make transparent what they are doing during their first days and weeks on the job and why. For equity-focused leaders, in addition, transparency requires being explicit about race, racism, and racial equity from the start. When leaders are transparent about their commitment to anti-racism from the beginning, they increase the chances that, together with the communities they serve, they can come to understand the real problems that stand in the way of progress.

Transparency also helps to build trust, especially with those who mistrust the organization. Students, parents, staff members, and community members will ask themselves: Will the new leader show me respect by listening to me? Will the new leader show me personal regard by going out of their way to see me? Will the new leader demonstrate competence early on? Will the new leader demonstrate personal integrity by keeping their word and staying true to core values and commitments?[4] Every move either builds or reduces trust, and equity-focused leaders must design their entry plans accordingly.

Listening with Empathy and Cultivating Understanding

An essential aspect of equity-focused leadership entry is deep listening, focused on seeking out and centering the voices of marginalized groups who are often not heard. Not only does the act of listening build trust and produce healing, but it also leads to a more nuanced understanding of the way the organization works in relationship to the community it serves. It is critical to seek understanding of the organization's technical systems, structures, and routines as well as its relational ways of working—the way information flows, the nature of relationships, and how people talk about the organization and its community.[5] In other words, the equity-focused leader must listen with ears, eyes, and heart for clues about how things work and the real organizational culture, far beyond what is written on paper.

Just as crucial for equity-focused entry is how the leader interprets the information gathered during those first months on the job. Data analysis is vital because the way we present, analyze, and interpret data can oversimplify the issues, reinforce stereotypes, and lead to shallow problem definitions and faulty solutions. Ivory Toldson, a professor at Howard University, insists that we start with "good data," then conduct "thoughtful analysis" to produce "compassionate understanding."[6] Most importantly, data analysis during leadership entry should ensure that the people behind the numbers inform collective sensemaking. Doing so will help the leader accurately identify the real equity-focused problems and begin to iterate potential solutions.

Changing the Narrative and Galvanizing for Action

In a typical formal leadership entry process, leaders share back what they think they have learned. But equity-focused leaders not only align their message, their audience, and their medium, they take advantage of their entry to communicate a new and genuine narrative focused on assets. Leadership entry offers us the opportunity to practice what Kim Scott calls "radical candor," the ability to challenge a person, or a community, directly with love and care.[7] In other words, equity-focused leaders use their entry to speak the truth and "speak to the future," focusing on possibilities.[8] Language matters, and it is crucial that leaders disrupt negative narratives from the start, especially about youth of color and their families.

Finally, leadership entry done well creates momentum, so new leaders often move seamlessly into strategy development after gathering information and insight about the organization. Equity-focused leaders, however, will ensure that the planning process is anchored to a vision worth pursuing, fosters collective responsibility for the organization's problems and solutions, and is responsive to complexity. That requires being explicit about problems rooted in racism, and allowing strategy, sometimes through intentional prototyping and testing, to emerge from the ground up.

Self and Communal Care

Finally, equity-focused leadership entry requires an emphasis on self and communal care at every stage. Caring is important because leadership change is a disruptive event despite its hope and possibility. Staff may feel uneasy, uncertain that their voices will be heard and valued based on past experiences. The community may be wary of the new leader's ability to follow through on commitments given past disappointments. The leader is often so busy that self-care is an afterthought. Equity-focused leaders, however, recognize that leadership entry done well surfaces unresolved pain and that hearing painful stories can be retraumatizing for the leader, too, especially leaders of color.[9] Anticipating the time and space necessary to hold and process these conversations, and to make room for emotion, is critical for everyone, including the leader. The act of listening, sensemaking, and action planning, however, can produce healing if done with love, care, and compassion. At minimum, a new leader should plan an entry process that causes no harm, especially to those who have been historically harmed the most. At its best, the process can result in the healing necessary for real change to occur.

TYPICAL COMPONENTS

In addition to these framework dimensions, we suggest leaders plan their entry with a few typical phases in mind (see figure 1.2).[10] These phases (and the suggested steps within) do not have to be done in chronological order; iteration is necessary, and sometimes steps happen simultaneously. It is also important to note that while leadership entry is often mapped out over the first ninety to one hundred days on the job, it can be shorter or longer depending on context. The key is transparency about your goals and process. Through every phase

FIGURE 1.2 Leadership Entry Phases

PHASE 1 REFLECT	PHASE 2 LISTEN AND LEARN	PHASE 3 PLAN TO ACT
• Reflect on identity • Explore context • Gather available data	• Set goals and introduce yourself • Gather data through engagement • Share in sensemaking • Communicate	• Articulate shared vision • Identify root causes • Develop strategy • Commit to inquiry

and step, no matter the order or the length of time, a leader is paying keen attention to themselves and their community's reactions, adjusting as they go. Here we lay them out with some distinguishing features for the equity-focused leader.

Phase 1: Reflect on Self and Context

The entry process often begins before the official start date. During this phase, it is helpful to reflect on identity in relation to the local context, convene key advisers to gain essential insight into historical and political context, and pressure-test the specifics of the draft entry plan. It is also an excellent time to gather various existing data about organizational ways of working and outcomes. At this stage, the leader's objective is to "see the system" so that they are ready for listening, learning, and sensemaking.[11]

Phase 2: Listen and Learn

Set goals and introduce yourself. As the official start date arrives, the leader will want to plan their introduction. A new leader typically describes why they are excited about the work, shares something personal about who they are and how it informs their approach, expresses their core values including their commitment to racial equity, and shares their leadership entry goals. The objective is to be transparent and begin the process of building trust.

Gather data through engagement. Before beginning the process of listening and learning, it is essential to define and communicate the inquiry questions that will drive the leader's data gathering. From there, the leader will decide on the information that can help answer those questions, including data gathered through engagement. The objective is to listen deeply to multiple perspectives about how the organization works and its impact, emphasizing nondominant voices.

Share in sensemaking. Once the leader has gathered relevant data, they must determine how to make sense of it, and the way one makes meaning of the data must be intentional. Leaders must discern what data to look at, how it should be displayed, and who should be involved in collaborative sensemaking. The leader's objective is to develop a deep understanding of the problems the organization and community face, and to form ideas about possible solutions.

Communicate. After the leader has made sense of that data, they will share what they have learned honestly, in a way that fosters reflection, inspires collective action, and disrupts stereotypes about students and families of color. The objective is to highlight what is possible with a focus on community assets, promote a shared understanding of the real equity-focused problems that stand in the way, and garner support for addressing them.

Phase 3: Plan to Act

For some, creating an action plan based on findings is the next logical step, and it may even be critical for building credibility as a leader. For others, it is not. Either way, it is crucial to think about using the entry process to galvanize for action in a complex environment. Knowing how to connect, inspire, and spur others toward increased leadership for equity is an integral part of leadership entry that can form the foundation for years to come.

In the following chapters, we explore each dimension, drawing out tangible examples, emphasizing the implications and skills needed to bring this dimension of the work to life, and offering a set of reflective questions for each leader's personal planning. We have also created a comprehensive reflective planning tool to help leaders plan their entry with attention to the framework dimensions (see appendix D). In all, we believe that the Entry for Equity framework, along with the reflective planning tool, will set up equity-focused leaders for success in ways that we have not seen previously. To lead for racial equity in schools, school systems, and related organizations, we must embrace this more nuanced set of knowledge, skills, and dispositions. By doing so, we can set the stage to work with our communities for the change our youth deserve.

CHAPTER 2

UNDERSTANDING SELF

It is important for all of us to appreciate where we come from and how that history has really shaped us in ways that we might not understand.

—SONIA SOTOMAYOR

One of the major themes that emerged during our empathy interviews with new leaders is that leadership entry offers an opportunity to communicate who you are and your core values.[1] Clarifying and communicating your "why" from the beginning is crucial. Equally important, however, is building self-awareness of your frames of reference, testing your assumptions and biases, and understanding your relationship to power. While leaders are often asked to focus from the start on changing structures, systems, and processes to get results, an equity-focused leader's approach begins with an understanding of self and one's multiple identities.

Scholar and clinical psychologist Beverly Tatum says, "The concept of identity is a complex one, shaped by individual characteristics, family dynamics, historical factors, and social and political contexts. Who am I? The answer depends in large part on who the world around me says I am."[2] While racial identity is often paramount in the US, she further explains that it "will be mediated by other dimensions of oneself: male, female, or transgender; young or old; wealthy, middle-class, or poor; gay, lesbian, bisexual, or heterosexual; able-bodied or with disabilities; Christian, Muslim, Jewish, Buddhist, Hindu, or atheist."[3] Our identities are multifaceted, and our understanding of our identity changes depending on our surroundings.

The literature on culturally responsive school leadership in education affirms the importance of understanding one's identity and developing critical consciousness.[4] Doing so will help the leader not only see the system they lead more objectively, including the inequities that negatively affect the youth they serve, but it will help test their personal frames of reference so that they can change that reality. This is important because our individual actions can either serve to maintain forms of inequity or to challenge them. As leadership experts Ronald Heifetz and Marty Linsky remind us, experienced leaders have "most certainly had some part in creating any existing problem and in failing to address that problem in the past."[5] Ensuring our actions lead to the change we desire requires expanding our frames of reference and seeing things anew.

The National Equity Project's "Liberatory Design Mindsets" offer helpful prompts for the examination of identity in advance of leadership entry, as leadership entry requires design.[6] The mindsets can be used to invoke personal values, along with self- and system awareness, to guide a leader's approach to leadership entry. Here we introduce three mindsets that we think are especially important for reflection, and we describe how they can be helpful before designing your leadership entry process.[7]

- *Practice self-awareness.* "Who we are determines how we design. Looking in the 'mirror' reveals what we see, how we relate, and how our perspectives impact our practice."[8] Leaders are more than their titles and job descriptions. They are human beings with unique lived experiences that influence the way they see the world, for better or worse. Leaders who practice self-awareness not only come to understand their own frames and unpack them, but they come to understand the frames of others and therefore more deeply understand the needs, desires, and experiences of people and communities they support. In leadership entry, this reflection on identity in relationship to the people we serve can open up new paths for inquiry, routines for checking assumptions, and opportunities to build more humanizing and authentic relationships from the start. Ask yourself: Who am I? Who are the people I serve?

- *Work to transform power.* "Explore structures and opportunities for interactions in which power is shared, not exercised."[9] Power, in the sense of the ability to do something or to direct or influence people and circumstances, is not evenly distributed.[10] In traditional leadership roles and organizations, there is usually an imbalance, tilted toward dominant groups. Further, power is held by just a small number of people, typically those with the most privilege, who make decisions on behalf of the majority and often out of public view. It is critical for leaders, then, to consider how they themselves are situated to power so that they can design a leadership entry process that disrupts power dynamics and creates new opportunities for transparency, shared decision-making, and influence. Ask yourself: How am I situated relative to power?

- *Recognize oppression.* "Learn to see how oppression, in its many forms, has shaped designs that lead to inequity."[11] Leaders must unpack their own personal experiences with oppression (individual, interpersonal, and systemic) to recognize how it impacts the way they view themselves and their context.[12] For White leaders, this may require examining internalized superiority and racial privilege, which can manifest in microaggressions and expressions of White fragility.[13] For leaders of color, this may require examining internalized oppression, which can manifest as negative thoughts and feelings about one's own social identity group and result in self-destructive behaviors, like imposter syndrome and stereotype threat.[14] For every leader, recognizing systemic oppression—how the system needs to change, not those who are oppressed—is critical. Ask yourself: How is oppression at play?

One overarching and devastating phenomenon—a common experience here in the US that influences our sense of self, the way power works, and the way oppression plays out—is White supremacy. Scholar Frances Lee Ansley defines it as the "political, economic and cultural system in which whites overwhelmingly control power and material resources," as well as ideas of White superiority, both conscious and unconscious.[15] White supremacy is a shared culture into which we all have been conditioned, and it is sometimes hard to see, no matter our racial identities. We unknowingly reinforce the taken-for-granted systems, routines, and ways of working that constitute that culture when left unexamined. Becoming more keenly aware of ourselves, our relationship to power, and our experience with oppression can help leaders change the dominant culture in powerful ways.

In this chapter, we'll examine the leadership entry of Dr. Nancy Gutiérrez, president and CEO of the Leadership Academy, a national nonprofit that focuses on building the capacity of educational leaders to dismantle systemic inequities in schools and create culturally responsive learning environments for every single student.[16] Nancy's entry story will provide insight into how her identity influenced her early leadership moves. We'll then analyze her approach to leadership entry with attention to self-awareness, power, and oppression, share some implications for the design of your own leadership entry, and offer a skill to practice.

LEADING FROM WITHIN

Nancy Gutiérrez spent most of her career as a teacher and principal in her hometown of East San Jose, California.[17] She experienced firsthand the challenges of growing up and teaching in a community with limited access to opportunities, and she understood deeply the needs and desires of the people who lived there. She was also aware of the unhealthy narrative that was told about East San Jose and communities like it, a story that perpetuated and reinforced negative and harmful stereotypes.

There were people in her life from childhood to adulthood, however, that helped her keep that unhealthy discourse at bay. Nancy's greatest teacher was her mother. Saturday mornings growing up, for example, she would take Nancy and her five siblings around the neighborhood, cleaning up any visible garbage, especially at the local schools, which taught Nancy important lessons about humility and service but also the importance of taking care of your home community. Later, it was Mr. Lovelace, her eighth-grade teacher, who helped her find her voice and passion for learning. He facilitated class discussions that made Nancy and her classmates feel seen. As Nancy says years later, "He pulled out our gifts and challenged us to challenge our assumptions and test ideas." She would take these lessons with her as a future educator. And later in life, when attending graduate school for her doctorate, she met Irma Zardoya, a Puerto Rican Bronx native who had dedicated her career to her home community and was currently serving as the CEO of the (then) NYC Leadership Academy. Irma would become her mentor and guide.

Nancy first learned about Irma when reading a Harvard case study about her leadership, and when she met her at a conference, they immediately connected and scheduled a lunch date. As another Latina leader in education whose leadership stance reflected authenticity and pride in her identity, Irma would provide Nancy with a space of affirmation and personal reflection, providing steady assurance that Nancy was well prepared to do the work, even when Nancy couldn't see it for herself. Eventually, Irma persuaded Nancy to transition to a role at the NYC Leadership Academy where she would be able to facilitate leadership development at the national level. And when Irma retired, she put Nancy forward to the board of directors as the candidate for president and CEO. Dario Collado of the Hispanic Heritage Foundation, a dear friend of Nancy's, says, "When you take the elevator up in life, you should always send it back down for others to follow." This mantra described the impact and importance of Irma's mentorship and guidance.

It was a great privilege for Nancy to follow in Irma's footsteps and to build on her legacy, charged with expanding the organization's national presence and deepening its impact and focus on equity. While the focus on equity seemed like a good fit, given her lived and professional experience, she wondered if she had the right profile to be the face of the organization with funders, especially the White power brokers who dominate the philanthropic space. She struggled at first as a result, feeling like she would have to give up a little bit of herself to fit the mold, whether that meant straightening her curly hair or giving up the big hoop earrings that she proudly embraced and celebrated in other spaces.

Her struggle with showing up as her authentic self didn't last too long. Not only did she realize that she didn't have to fit that mold, but in time, she could break the mold, too. She recalls her very first staff meeting as CEO of the Leadership Academy. The planning team carefully structured an agenda that included a data review about the state of equitable practice internal to the organization. This agenda led to opportunities for staff to share their truths, experiences, and stories, most of them painful, but the conversation was going over the allotted time. As a team, however, they decided to stay present in the space of sharing, reflecting, and listening. She shared what it took to resist the urge to go back to the agenda: "I had to fight against a perfectionist ideology that the meeting needed to go exactly as planned. I soon realized that the disappointment stemmed from my ego as opposed to what I knew was the right thing to do." After the meeting, she recalls receiving feedback from a member of her team who said it was one of the best meetings that he had ever attended—that it was the first time, ever, in his history with the organization, that such a space had been created for people to speak their truth in an authentic way.

The experience also inspired her to leverage her own stories more. She began to share more about her life growing up in East San Jose as a way of demonstrating why the work they did was important. She recalls a meeting with one of the founding board members, who shared that her interview was the first time that he understood what equity really meant, because she shared her story and how her identity and experience was impacted. He confessed to having gotten stuck in the multiple definitions of equity and the lack of personalization. She knew that storytelling was a lever for change, internally and externally, and that the more that she talked about her past experiences and the people who helped shaped her identity, the more that she could help bring people along. On the first day of her tenure in 2018, she released "The Answer Is in the Room."

THE ANSWER IS IN THE ROOM
—NANCY GUTIÉRREZ

The answer is in the room.

Growing up in East San Jose, CA, it was rare to hear someone say those words in a classroom, parent gathering, or town meeting. Instead, consultants would cycle in and out of our "low-income," "low-performing," "dangerous" schools, with good intentions for improving them—without knowing much about the strengths that existed within us as a community. Outsiders hoped to make change to us, not with us. They didn't see that the answers lay within the families, young people, and educators in the community—in the "room."

I am proud today to become the next President & CEO of the NYC Leadership Academy, an organization that deeply believes in and has faithfully lived by that mantra. In each community we support—whether a predominately African American district in Cleveland or schools supporting primarily Indigenous students in Nevada—we always begin by asking local educators and communities, "What are your challenges and ideas? What are your values? What do the leaders within your context need to know and be able to do to improve learning for every single student?"

We take the time to deeply understand context.

We build authentic relationships with leaders charged with moving the work forward.

continued

And we look for the answers in the room.

The leaders I have looked up to throughout my life, who have inspired me and others to be our better selves and do our best work, lived by this belief. My greatest teacher, my mother, would take me and my five siblings to pick up litter and scrub out graffiti in our neighborhood on Saturday mornings. It was never a question that we would be a part of creating solutions to the challenges that sat outside our front door.

When I was in 8th grade, almost every teacher requested that I not be in their class because they had heard I was a "troublemaker." But Mr. Lovelace sought me out. He believed in me. He knew that the answers lay within me. Over that year he built me up, ignited within me the love for learning I always had but had never been encouraged to explore. He helped me find my voice, encouraging me to write my story for a state-level competition and to advocate against policies I believed were unfair to youth of color living with limited resources like myself—from school uniform policies to CA Proposition 187 which sought to restrict access for undocumented families to health care and public education.

After college, I returned to my home community to teach. On my first day, a teacher colleague expressed her surprise that I had come from the neighborhood, and curiosity at whether my classmates, friends, and family members had ended up teen mothers or in jail. Mr. Lovelace, on the other hand, sent me flowers with a note that read, simply, "Congratulations, Maestra."

Wanting to be a part of finding the answers in the room, I followed Maria Vizcarra, the mother of one of my students, into a house meeting where parents across our community were rallying behind a new vision for our public schools. It was my honor to ultimately become the founding principal of the middle school they dreamed of in that room that evening. Indeed, the continued success of the three new small schools we launched in East San Jose was born from the fact that the answers came from within the community.

While at The Leadership Academy, we have put a stake in the ground around equity since our inception 15 years ago, part of our work moving forward must be to ensure that "equity" does not become an empty word, that it has depth and real meaning.

We know that this work cannot be done in isolation, so we are committed to developing and supporting educational leaders in ways that ensure that all students, regardless of race, class, ethnicity, or culture, have access to the learning opportunities and resources they need to become leaders themselves—to find the answers within, to hold themselves accountable to the changes they wish to see.

> I have seen firsthand how the impact of one person, like Mr. Lovelace or Maria Vizcarra, can become exponential through strong leadership. What an absolute privilege it is to support leaders across the country to solve persistent problems—by tapping into the answers that lie within the room.
>
> *Source*: Nancy Gutiérrez, "The Answer Is in the Room," Leadership Academy, September 30, 2018, https://www.leadershipacademy.org/blog/we-always-look-for-the-answers-in-the-room.

Nancy recognized that during her entry it was critical not to dismiss the value of her identity nor forget the experiences and stories of those who came before her. The collective genius of her family and community shaped who she was. She also recognized the importance of having a trusted mentor and sounding board who helped her every step of the way. Those experiences, stories, and support guided her leadership moves, ensuring that her own identity was seen and celebrated throughout the process.

OUR ANALYSIS

We hope this story demonstrates the importance of identity in leadership entry. In this section, we'll delve more into the opportunities Nancy Gutiérrez embraced and the challenges she faced with a focus on the critical mindsets of self-awareness, power, and oppression.

Practice Self-Awareness

Nancy's identity as a Xicana had always been central in her roles as teacher and principal in East San Jose. She was clear on who she served and why, and she carried the stories of her community with her. During her entry, Nancy was able to leverage those stories with other stakeholders, like her board and members of her staff, to help expand their perspectives about the kind of leadership that was needed in schools. This understanding of self and core values made it easy for her to connect to her equity-focused charge.

In this new job, however, which also required that she continue to expand the organization's national presence beyond New York City, there were moments during her entry where she felt like she had to give up part of herself to be accepted. While she had safe places to process this through honest and transparent dialogue, she was still tentative at first about whether she could express herself openly in the new job. Thinker/organizer Aysa Gray writes about these White-dominant standards of professionalism:

> These values, established over time as history and fact, have been used to create the narrative of white supremacy that underpins professionalism today, playing out in the hiring, firing, and day-to-day management of workplaces around the world. The story unfolds many ways: in white and Western standards of dress and hairstyle (straightened hair, suits but not saris, and burqa and beard bans in some countries); in speech, accent, word choice, and communication (never show emotion, must sound "American," and must speak standard white English); in scrutiny (black employees are monitored more closely and face more penalties as a result); and in attitudes toward timeliness and work style.[18]

What Nancy experienced initially was what many leaders of color experience in White-dominant spaces, where their authentic selves are not accepted or respected. This was a major challenge for Nancy during her entry, but she decided to give herself and the organization time. While building her credibility as CEO, she simultaneously began to bring more of herself to the job. Eventually, she found she could express and celebrate her cultural identity completely. She also understood that by doing so, those who worked with her could more confidently do the same.

Work to Transform Power

Nancy's role as CEO of one of the country's most prominent leadership development organizations required her to be in the front most times, carrying the vision and mission of the organization. During her entry, she was constantly acknowledging the privilege that came with the role and making sure she was paying attention to those who had been harmed by the system that she was now leading. She acknowledged and raised the voices and experiences of staff and the people they served. She published everything she heard during her listening tours. She created new systems and structures for staff to connect to the work in meaningful ways. Mostly, she took advantage of her positionality to disrupt existing power structures by centering nondominant voices, increasing transparency, and getting people out of their silos.

There were also spaces and communities, however, where she could not only not be herself immediately, but where Nancy did not yet have access to power, particularly with funders, who were often White men and women. In these spaces, she recalls feeling overlooked and undervalued, treated like she was in a support role even though she shared the same positional authority. It created for her the constant need to prove that she belonged, especially during her first year, whether it was through communicating her connections or credentials. She admits that she had to work harder to earn a place at this particular table, and now that she is there, she not only demands the respect she deserves but uses her seat to disrupt and call out the power dynamics in the philanthropic space as well.

Recognize Oppression

Early on, Nancy was able to disrupt the internalized oppression that distorted how she engaged with her staff during her first meeting as the new leader. There was an intentional pause and connection to her own experiences that allowed her to see and understand what was happening in the moment; people were hurting. Her first inclination was to get her team back on track and power through the agenda, an expectation of the dominant culture, but she quickly realized this was not the time. While many leaders have been ingrained in this perfectionist ideology, Nancy decided to pause and allow for people to heal and share the hurt, disappointment, and pain associated with their experiences. The same was true for the organization's leadership cabinet, which had to engage in intentional healing processes to liberate themselves to truly lead in authentic ways. As a result, she created an authentic partnership between herself and her team. She was quickly able to reflect and recognize that this blind spot could have been detrimental to building trust between herself and her staff, and that it was only through showing up and leading with vulnerability that she would truly earn trust and create the conditions needed to become an equitable organization over time.

IMPLICATIONS FOR LEADERS

Understanding yourself is crucial for authentic and equity-focused leadership from the start. In this next section, we share several implications for the design of your leadership entry, with a focus on methods to build self-awareness and reflective practice.

Identify an Accountability Partner or Coach

For new leaders, identifying someone early on who can be a critical thought partner during entry can quickly mitigate mistakes and provide a safe space for self-reflection. That's because people generally avoid direct feedback, even when it is good for them. Psychiatrist Jay Jackman and Professor Myra Strober write: "Psychologists have a lot of theories about why people are so sensitive to hearing about their own imperfections. Whatever the cause of our discomfort, most of us have to train ourselves to seek feedback and listen carefully when we hear it. The very threat of critical feedback often leads us to practice destructive, maladaptive behaviors that negatively affect not only our work but the overall health of our organizations."[19]

An accountability partner acts as a trusted colleague who is responsible for making sure that you are operating with integrity, in alignment with your values, and with knowledge of your blind spots. Finding an accountability partner who is familiar with the landscape can also be beneficial. They can come in the form of a formal/informal mentor, a local leader, or a trusted colleague from within the community or organization. Marshall Goldsmith, former executive and one of the top executive leadership coaches in the world, suggests that you find opportunities with an accountability partner to receive feedback weekly in a two- to three-minute conversation.[20] The questions could be simple: What did you observe about how I showed up? What was the impact? What should I consider doing differently or continue to leverage? These quick conversations are not intended to be formal. The idea is to be present, listen, and reflect on the feedback without justifying your actions.

An executive coach can also be extremely beneficial, especially if they come with a level of expertise similar to the leader's role and if their coaching philosophy supports the leader's external and internal needs. For leaders of color, finding an executive leadership coach of color can be especially beneficial for navigating and influencing workplaces that stifle authenticity. In her article "Cracking the Code That Stalls People of Color," Sylvia Ann Hewlett states: "'Cracking the code' of executive presence presents unique challenges for professionals of color because standards for appropriate behavior, speech, attire, demand they suppress or sacrifice aspects of their cultural identity."[21] The reality is that many of these discriminatory standards still exist in organizations and school systems across the country. Executive leadership coaches of color can help leaders of color manage the expectations of others and tap into their true authentic selves.

Assess Your Leadership Style

It is important for leaders to reflect on their identities, but they should also reflect on their leadership styles, and we all tend to lean on some styles more than others, for better or worse. We believe it's critical for leaders to communicate with their teams their leadership style preferences for transparency and trust building, but even more, they should ask for their feedback to make sure that their preferred styles match organizational needs. If they don't, an adjustment can be made early on. That's because while we all have our preferences, we can adjust our leadership styles to match the needs of the organization at any given time. One excellent resource for doing so is the inventory of leadership styles developed by Daniel Goleman.

LEADERSHIP STYLES THAT PRODUCE A POSITIVE WORK CLIMATE AND OUTSTANDING PERFORMANCE

- *Visionary* leaders articulate a shared mission and give long-term direction.
- *Participative* leaders get consensus to generate new ideas and build commitment.
- *Coaching* leaders foster personal and career development.
- *Affiliative* leaders create trust and harmony.

Source: Daniel Goleman, "What's Your Leadership Style?," Korn Ferry, https://www.kornferry.com/insights/this-week-in-leadership/whats-your-leadership-style.

In addition to discussing leadership style up front, also consider soliciting feedback from direct team members on how they are experiencing you as a leader a few months into your tenure. Equity-focused leaders might expand this feedback to include friends, colleagues, peers, and in some cases, members of the larger community who will have different perspectives. This will provide you with a holistic picture of what's needed and required of your leadership early on. These intentional feedback loops can also be conducted annually to ensure that leaders change their style based on what is needed, as context is fluid.

Continually Pause and Reflect

Ralph Waldo Emerson said, "In each pause, I hear the call." It's in our time of pausing and slowing down that we can reconnect with who we are, who we want to be, and the impact we want to have. One way of creating intentional spaces to pause and reflect is to build uninterrupted time within your work schedule. This could vary based on your weekly routines, but it's usually most impactful if you start at the beginning or end of the workweek. Mondays could begin with some form of meditation like yoga or prayer, and Fridays could be committed time for personal reflection. Below are a few questions to consider during this quiet time:

- What did I experience this week that surfaced heavy emotions for me?
- What was the impact on myself and others?
- What actions are required to self-correct or heal?

A SKILL: DEVELOPING YOUR LEADERSHIP STORY

Before you begin the process of leadership entry, we suggest that you develop a leadership story to articulate your personal values, connections, and hopes for the organization. This story can be used in various forms during your leadership entry and will serve you well for years to come. Table 2.1 presents a helpful framework for developing a leadership story that informs people of who you are, why you are here, and what they can expect from you.

FINAL REFLECTION

For each of us, leadership entry required that we knew ourselves and our values. This understanding informed how we engaged with others with authenticity and influenced how we interpreted the system

TABLE 2.1 Leadership story development reflective questions

WHO AM I?
What personal or professional experiences contribute to who you are today? What values did these experiences create?

WHY AM I HERE?
What personal connections can you make to the organization's mission/vision? Why do you want to lead here, now?

WHAT CAN PEOPLE EXPECT FROM ME?
How does who you are and your reasons for taking the job affect the way you will lead? What is your approach to leadership?

we were part of. It also required that we become more aware of our biases and blind spots, which surfaced insecurities and fears, but also served as a powerful source for learning. Self-reflection, however, isn't just a one-and-done thing for those entering a new role or context. For equity-focused leaders, it is a practice that lasts a lifetime. It takes courage, but slowing down to understand yourself and how your multiple identities impact what you see and how you engage helps mitigate the unpredictability of equity-focused change.

As you plan for your leadership entry, consider these reflective questions:

- Who am I? What are my values? How does my lived and professional experience influence the way I view the work and my role?
- Who are the people I serve? What are their values? What do they expect from me?
- How am I perceived? How will that affect what people share with me?
- What are my biases? How do I maintain awareness of my biases and challenge them to see this organization and the community it serves more authentically?
- What do I need to lead with authenticity?

CHAPTER 3

UNDERSTANDING CONTEXT

*The better we understand how identities and power work
together from one context to another, the less likely our
movements for change are to fracture.*

—KIMBERLÉ WILLIAMS CRENSHAW

The first question we asked in our empathy interviews with new
leaders was, "What were the circumstances surrounding your hiring?"[1] One Black female superintendent told us she was promoted
from within after her predecessor was ousted due to a scandal. She
was charged with restoring integrity through transparency. A White
male superintendent told us he was hired after an initial failed search
to fill his longtime predecessor's shoes. He was tasked with building
on his legacy. A Black male superintendent shared that he was recruited from out of state after the previous leader's contract was not
renewed. He was hired to fix a broken system with urgency. In every
case, the leader was situated within a particular context.

So in addition to knowing ourselves and how our identities
may influence the way we lead, new leaders must become keenly
aware of the context they are entering from the beginning. This is
critical even when starting a new leadership role in the same organization, because an understanding of context ought to influence
leadership moves as well. But what exactly is "context"? According
to the *Merriam-Webster Dictionary*, it is "the interrelated conditions
in which something exists or occurs."[2] A new leader must quickly
discern the who, what, where, when, why, and how of the place they
work and the community in which it is situated so that they can effectively negotiate and execute on their charge.

Education leadership professor Rachel Roegman, in her study of equity-focused leadership in context, suggests that we ought to think of these interrelated conditions as personal, organizational, occupational, and social, which are helpful categories for our exploration of the subject.[3]

- The *personal context* describes who we are, our racial, gender, and other identities; our backgrounds; and our motivations, both personal and professional.[4] In our experience, personal context includes our family situations and our personal histories with the community we serve as well.
- The *organizational context* describes how the organization works, with a focus on systems, structures, and routines, including lines of authority and structures for decision-making.[5] For us, organizational context includes understanding key technical aspects of the organization, like data and information systems, but must also include relational aspects of the organization, including the state of trusting relationships between people.
- The *occupational context* describes how the leader was trained in graduate school or through other professional organizations and is influenced to think about the work by their colleagues.[6] In our experience, this includes how our professional trajectories influence the way we think about the work.
- The *social context* describes the beliefs and ideologies at play in the larger community in which the organization is situated, including how systemic racism and oppression manifest.[7] We also believe that social context must include attention to history. It is critical for equity-focused leaders to understand not just the current state, but the history of oppression, opportunity, and racial and social justice leadership in their communities so that they can build on it.[8]

Understanding context is important because effective leadership entry requires what education leadership scholars Paul Bredeson, Hans Klar, and Olof Johansson call "context-responsive leadership." In their study of superintendent leadership, for example, they state: "Variations in context constitute opportunities as well as constraints to an individual's capacity to motivate and engage others in collaborative efforts to achieve organizational goals."[9] It is important to assess the context for both opportunities and constraints so that the leader can both manage the complex environment in which they are situated and influence it. Even more, while understanding context is critical during leadership entry, context is dynamic; it is always changing. Effective leaders must be attuned to context from the start and stay attuned to changes in the environment throughout their tenure.

Most importantly, your entry period offers your first, and perhaps best, opportunity to learn about the context in which you will do the work. In this chapter, we will share the leadership entry story of Dr. Sonja Santelises, CEO of the Baltimore City Public Schools, who began her superintendency in 2016. We chose to highlight Sonja's entry because of her attention to the Baltimore context during her entry, which she believes set herself up for a strong start. We then analyze her work, pulling out critical themes that may be instructive for leadership entry planning, summarize a few actionable next steps, and suggest a critical skill to practice. Ultimately, we hope you will come away with some clarity about the importance of context and how to put this dimension into action.

LEADERSHIP ENTRY AFTER CRISIS

Sonja Santelises temporarily left the Baltimore City Public Schools (City Schools) and her role as the chief academic officer (CAO) when her boss, then CEO Andrés Alonso, resigned in 2013 and a new CEO took over. With twenty-five years of experience under her belt as a professional developer, school and district leader, and superintendent coach, all in urban settings, she had established a strong reputation in Baltimore in a short period of time. She brought coherence to the district's instructional program, focusing on instructional methods and rigorous content, which contributed to the improvement of student outcomes on state exams and graduation rates after years of low performance.

Given the leadership change, however, she decided to leave the district that she had grown to love to take a position at the Education Trust, a national think tank where she could serve as an advocate for youth of color nationwide, while remaining in Baltimore as a resident and mother to three school-age children who attended the public schools there.

During her brief hiatus from City Schools, much was happening in Baltimore, but the death of Freddie Gray in April of 2015 and the months-long protests that followed were the most consequential. Freddie Gray, a twenty-five-year-old Black man, was arrested for having possession of a knife. He then suffered severe injuries while in police custody, shackled and transported unbuckled in a police van.[10] His death resulted in waves of protests, starting with an incident involving a large group of students from Baltimore's Frederick Douglass High School who were left at a bus station with no transportation and then confronted by police.[11]

Sonja remembers how the media characterized the young people of Baltimore at the time, former students from schools she personally visited as the CAO. The images that went viral portrayed Baltimore's students as unlawful thugs, throwing rocks and bottles at police officers, when nothing could be further from the truth. As described in a *Baltimore* magazine article in September 2017, "Nothing frustrate[d] Santelises more than hearing the district and its students maligned."[12]

Later that year, as the trial for the first officer was ending and a verdict was soon to be announced, the school district, sensing another wave of student protests, threatened its students with disciplinary action for walking out of class to participate. While the intention was to keep students safe, the district response was received by many as tone-deaf and unsupportive of students' desire to advocate for change. In a *Washington Post* article on December 15, 2015, the ACLU president in Maryland stated that the school district administration "assumes that students only want to express their emotions, not rational views about the conduct of police and lack of accountability, and it misses an opportunity to affirmatively engage students who want to be politically engaged on these issues." The experience further reduced the Black community's trust in a school district administration that seemed disconnected from the pain and suffering of young people across the city. Before long, in the spring of 2016 and only two years into his role, the CEO was ousted by the school board.[13]

When the school board president came to Sonja soon after, exploring her interest in coming back to City Schools as its new CEO, she was not entirely surprised. She was also conscious of the precarious circumstances, as it had only been a year since Freddie Gray's death, and trust was low. Nevertheless, she was motivated by the call to action, which offered an opportunity to represent Baltimore and its public schools in a much different light, to heal, and to rebuild trust. As long as the board also understood that she would be actively balancing and integrating her important roles as a wife and a mother, she would take it on, charged with putting the district back on track.

She shared, "It was clear that trust in institutions was at a low point. So it was essential to communicate and activate a partnership with the community in tangible and palpable ways."[14] As a result, she focused most of her early activities on more nuanced interactions and with much less fanfare than the typical new superintendent. She walked the streets of her community as a member of it, often participating in local events with her family. She rebuffed having a security detail trail her every move. She said, "If teachers and families have to walk these blocks, so do I." She also prioritized filling the family and community engagement position on her leadership team to give her more capacity to engage effectively from the start.

During her entry, she also prioritized meeting with the young people whose voices had been stifled, from incarcerated youth to student council presidents to LGBTQ+ youth, to get a sense of their hopes and dreams. She used her existing connections with community leaders to meet with people who might ordinarily be out of reach, like gang members and hard-to-reach parents, to better understand their personal aspirations and all that had stood in the way. And finally, she made sure to talk with community elders, those who could tell her stories of the powerful history of leadership for racial and social justice in Baltimore, a history that could inform the district's strategy with a focus on building from strength.

What she learned from these early interactions ultimately led to the identification of three major focus areas for the district, captured in the district's strategic plan called the *Blueprint for Success*—student wholeness, literacy, and leadership.[15]

FOCUS AREAS FROM THE *BLUEPRINT FOR SUCCESS*

Our students, families, staff members, and community stakeholders have shared their experiences of our schools, and they point to three areas with significant promise for ensuring our students' success:

- We need to know our students as unique people with unique experiences, talents, challenges, and social, emotional, and physical lives. By keeping the wholeness of our students in mind, hearing their voices, and building partnerships with their families and communities, we can ignite their passion for learning.
- We need to improve literacy teaching across all grades and subjects, and provide richer literacy experiences for all students. To meet and exceed high academic standards and access the opportunities they deserve, our students must be able to comprehend challenging content and express themselves powerfully.
- All staff members need to take leadership roles in connecting with, supporting, inspiring, and challenging students and contributing to their success.

Source: Baltimore City Public Schools website, https://www.baltimorecityschools.org/blueprint.

These three tenets arose in service of a larger idea: to be successful, students in Baltimore would need to be engaged in a new way, one that truly honored their humanity, their brilliance, and their possibility. It also provided clear direction at a critical time without being overly prescriptive, providing room for the community to learn and iterate together without getting bogged down in the bureaucracy. Looking back, Sonja appreciates the complexity of the Baltimore she entered, but mostly she is reminded that to lead the district forward she needed to see the community not as broken, but as resilient, powerful, and filled with promise.

OUR ANALYSIS

There is so much to learn from Sonja Santelises' entry into the Baltimore City Public Schools with attention to context. In this section we delve deeper into the personal, organizational, occupational, and social contexts that informed her early work there. In each section of our analysis, we will use additional examples that demonstrate both the constraints her context posed and the opportunities it afforded and how they informed her early leadership moves.[16]

Personal Context

As we mentioned in the last chapter, identity matters. While many identity descriptors will remain static throughout our lives, much of our personal context (which includes our motivations, our family situations, and our personal histories with the community we serve) changes. It affects how we view the work and to what extent we prioritize issues.

In this case, Sonja's identity as a Black woman, wife, and mother of three provided critical personal context that influenced the way she worked from day one. She was willing to take the job because of her personal connection to the community and the students of Baltimore and for no other reason. In *Baltimore* magazine she was quoted as saying to a group of funders, "Let me be real clear: I am not back here because I need a job. I am back here because of the kids and families of Baltimore."[17]

She was also unwilling to compromise her family's well-being for the job. For her, that would manifest in several ways early on. She and her husband would choose, for example, to live in a safe, middle-class neighborhood unapologetically, and she would protect her weekends to the extent possible to make time for her family. If there was a weekend event, she would try to integrate family time with her attendance whenever possible. But perhaps most important, she prioritized the establishment of an excellent leadership team early in her tenure, one with which she could share responsibility so that the district would not be overreliant on any one person. Instead of keeping her personal context out of sight, Sonja demonstrates how important it is that it was considered, discussed, and integrated into her approach to leadership from the beginning.

Organizational Context

The organizational context, which describes how the organization works, including the state of trusting relationships between people, certainly must be factored into a leader's moves in the first weeks and months on the job. This includes taking full stock of the priorities that were established by the former leader before making change.

For Sonja, perhaps the most critical factor regarding the organizational context was the ousting of the former superintendent and its impact on the organizational culture and the leadership team that she inherited. While in some ways following an ineffective leader can be easier because everything you do is likely to be deemed better by comparison, Sonja learned quickly that it was incredibly important not to disparage the former leader, even if some of their policies and approaches were ineffective.

Doing so poses too many risks. One major risk is the possibility that you will unknowingly dismantle good work. Sonja recognized, for example, the tremendous work that her predecessor did to re-build the arts, and she did not want to inadvertently undermine that progress. A new leader also runs the risk of knowingly halting prom-ising work, because of one's own skepticism, before fully understand-ing it. Her predecessor, for example, introduced the Community Schools model during his tenure, a school design in which the school functions as a hub for the community, shares leadership responsibil-ity with parents and community members, and coordinates needed services. While she was uncertain at first, the model proved to be critical in the long run, especially during the COVID-19 crisis. She learned a major lesson: "Don't just tear things down. Recognize what is good. And know it is just as important to give things time, to pay attention, and let things grow." Too often, new leaders are dismissive of the work of their predecessors and the team members who were associated with them, which creates initiative fatigue, reduced trust, and lost traction. Sonja chose instead to ask good questions, to build instead of dismantling, and to test assumptions every step of the way.

Occupational Context

Often overlooked is one's occupational context (past job experiences, training, and organizational affiliations), which certainly influences a new leader's work. These past experiences function as a lens through which one sees the organization, but they can also produce blind spots and assumptions that need to be tested.

Sonja, for example, knew going into her new role as CEO that she often viewed the work through the lens of an "academician." With degrees from Brown, Columbia, and Harvard, including a doc-torate from the Harvard Urban Superintendents Program, she was trained to focus on teaching and learning. Thankfully, her experi-ence starting a school in Brooklyn, New York, as well as her experi-ence heading up the NYC Algebra Project influenced her thinking about community involvement in education. Her motivation to be a superintendent was not about doing anything in any particular way, despite her knowledge about effective practices in education, but about principle-driven leadership that centered a commitment to young people, their families, and their communities. In this new context, viewing the work narrowly would prove problematic, and she had to work hard to broaden her lens.

One way she did so was to quietly, but not secretly, bring in a transition team of external experts, led by trusted colleagues affiliated with the Urban Superintendents Program, to help her expand her viewpoint, confirm hunches, and test assumptions. She focused much of this team's work on an analysis of the strength of her leadership team, which means she did not make many immediate changes. While Sonja has a strong instructional background, she knows that a superintendent is charged with the health of every dimension of a school district, and she needed partners who could help her execute. It was important not to overlook talent on the existing team and to fill gaps, where needed, in alignment with the emerging strategy.

Social Context

Finally, and perhaps most important, a new leader must consider the social context when entering a new leadership role: the beliefs and ideologies at play in the larger community, including how systemic racism and oppression manifest. Understanding this backdrop is essential for creating a shared vision of what is possible, a deep understanding of what stands in the way, and a strategy for getting there.

As Sonja described, "At the time of my entry, the city was in a place where the distrust of every institution within the city was palpable." She understood, however, that this wariness was not new, but the result of a long history of racial oppression in her community. One of her early steps was to go back, with educators across the school system, and understand the history of redlining in Baltimore, a practice used to segregate Black neighborhoods by denying services to residents like loans and insurance. Sonja explains, "We can't just do school absent of a knowledge of what the community has experienced, and how different communities have been impacted by a legacy around legislated, race-based distribution of resources." Understanding this history allowed her to communicate with the larger Baltimore community in a way that district leaders had not done before. It also gave her team insight into how to intentionally disrupt these historical patterns.

Just as important, she knew she needed to understand the history of racial justice leadership in Baltimore. She said, "In Baltimore, there are people who are still alive who remember when Frederick Douglass High School sent kids to Howard University Law. They remember when the schools taught art. To go after systemic racism without weaving in between the brilliance of communities, the resilience of communities, only perpetuates a mindset of victimhood. It can't just be about the pain, but the strength."

In Sonja's case, executing a full-on entry plan with a very public display of her meeting schedule was not the right move. She had to make context-specific leadership moves that preserved some semblance of work-life balance for her family while prioritizing authentic community engagement, healing, and relationship building. She had to craft a plan that would build on her community's strengths without disparaging or dismissing the good work that came before her. And she had to carefully build a powerful leadership team to execute on the new plan that emerged.

IMPLICATIONS FOR LEADERS

Michael Fullan, in his new edition of *Leading in a Culture of Change*, insists that leaders must have "deep contextual literacy" to be effective.[18] So in addition to thinking about context as nested and interrelated, we wanted to offer a few actionable implications for the design of your equity-focused leadership entry plan that will help increase your contextual literacy quickly.

Understand Your Charge

New leaders, especially equity-focused leaders, need to know why they were hired, negotiate the expectations for their performance, and assess the opportunities, risks, and constraints associated with meeting those expectations. This process starts before even accepting the job.

One of the equity leaders we spoke with emphasized how important it was to be cautious about saying yes. It is critical to know your core values and to ensure that the organization is right for you, especially if you are a leader of color leading for racial equity. The interview must go both ways. This is particularly important for female leaders of color, who, because of their relational skills, are often hired to clean up messy situations and then overscrutinized, setting them up for a precarious entry from the start.[19] Mid-level leaders, in our experience, also tend to have even more difficulties clarifying their job expectations up front.

Having a series of crucial conversations with your board, supervisor(s), and other key stakeholders, like key collaborators and colleagues, during the hiring process and extending through one's first weeks on the job, is key for shaping and clarifying expectations up front.

In his business book on leadership entry, Michael Watkins recommends the following crucial conversations to be had with your boss(es) and potentially other key stakeholders: the situation conversation, the expectations conversation, the style conversation, the resources conversation, and the personal development conversation.[20] For the equity-focused leader, however, we suggest that each of these conversations be done with race and equity at the center, as demonstrated by the sample equity-focused questions shown in table 3.1. Further, we believe there is a crucial conversation about resistance that must be initiated by new leaders who intend to lead for equity from the start. This conversation is critical for every leader, but especially for leaders of color and female leaders, who may experience resistance more acutely.

TABLE 3.1 Equity-focused leadership questions

CONVERSATION	OBJECTIVE	SAMPLE EQUITY-FOCUSED QUESTIONS
Situation conversation	To gain understanding of how they see the state of the organization	How do racial inequality and other forms of oppression currently manifest in the organization? What ways of working have been put in place to identify and dismantle it?
Expectations conversation	To clarify and negotiate what you are expected to accomplish	To what extent can I be explicit about my focus on racial equity?
Style conversation	To discuss how you will interact and your preferred methods of communication and decision-making	What will it look like for me to manage "up" about crucial equity issues?
Resources conversation	To negotiate critical resources to do the job well	Are current resources aligned with our equity priorities? What resources can I expect if I am being asked to lead for equity?
Personal development conversation	To identify support focused on personal and professional growth	Where are the places I can find community? Where can I process safely and get support?
Anticipated resistance conversation	To openly discuss the ways that resistance will manifest in the organization	What will resistance look like, sound like, feel like? What support (and even protection) can I expect from you?

Note: The first five conversations come from Michael D. Watkins, *The First 90 Days: Proven Strategies for Getting Up to Speed Faster and Smarter, Updated and Expanded* (Boston: Harvard Business Review Press, 2013).

Create an Advisory Group or Transition Team

We also believe that creating an advisory group or transition team can help early on. This group can help a leader gain understanding of social and historical context, or provide additional, objective insight into organizational context.

Several of the leaders we interviewed talked about how crucial it was to establish a "kitchen cabinet" early on in their tenure, an informal group of people who are both well-connected in the community and committed to serving as trusted and confidential advisers. Typically, these cabinet members represent different constituencies and points of view. They can provide connections to key players in the community and advice on how to show up as a leader. They can help a new leader understand the social context and the history of the place. They also can help shape the entry plan while it's still in development. For many leaders, the creation of a kitchen cabinet is not only a crucial early leadership move but forms a group that continues to meet as needed throughout the leader's tenure.

A transition team, on the other hand, is a hand-selected team of experts who can help gain additional understanding in identified areas of concern and present recommendations to the new leader, mainly focused on organizational context. If a leader chooses to use a transition team, it is important to think carefully about how the group will be perceived by the community at large, how they are paid, who is asked to participate, and how they go about their work. For example, we would advise that transition teams are carefully selected based on needed areas of expertise, that there is a mix of local and national experts, and that they are paid through external funds. In most situations, transition teams are not given a lot of attention but work more discreetly to make sense out of critical aspects of organizational capacity, systems, and structures.

Begin the Process of Assessing Your Team

If you manage a team, one of the things you will want to do early on is to begin to assess its strengths and weaknesses. In our opinion, the practice of fully replacing a team immediately is a mistake, unless there is evidence of rampant corruption. That is because your existing team will have deep contextual knowledge that you will need to understand the organization and its community. Too much change to the team too early can create unnecessary risk. In chapter 5, we will discuss the kinds of questions you will want to ask your team, but at the earliest stages of entry, you will want to begin thinking about what you need from the team to assess its strengths and gaps more easily.

TABLE 3.2 Career imprint questions

Cognitions	How have your past training and early career experiences influenced the way you see the world? How might that view help you assess the context you are entering? Where are your blind spots? Who do you need around you to help you test assumptions?
Capabilities	How have your past training and early career experiences helped you develop the skills you most rely on? What skills may be underdeveloped as a result? What skills do you need to work on, and who else will you rely on to fill your gaps?
Confidence	How have your past training and early career experiences influenced your sense of self-efficacy? Where are you overconfident? Underconfident? Who can you depend on to help you have a healthy sense of self-efficacy in the job?
Connections	How have your past training and early career experiences influenced your professional and social networks? Where are your connections strong? What kinds of networks do you tend to develop—those that are broad and diverse, or those that are more focused or narrow? Where are they weak? How can you strengthen them, and who else on your team can help?

Source: Monica C. Higgins, *Career Imprints: Creating Leaders Across an Industry* (San Francisco: Jossey-Bass, 2005).

One way to do this is for leaders to become more aware of their own "career imprints," a concept coined by Monica Higgins, a professor at the Harvard Graduate School of Education. That is because our training and the places we have worked, especially those early in our careers, have imprinted us with sets of capabilities, connections, confidence, and cognitions.[21] These career imprints will undoubtedly influence how a new leader makes sense of the organization and community it serves, and they can create blind spots. A leadership team should offer a well-rounded set of capabilities, knowledge, and insight aligned to its charge. As you consider your context, we encourage you to ask yourself the questions in table 3.2 and surface implications for future team formation and building.

A SKILL: POLITICAL MAPPING WITH AN EQUITY LENS

Finally, we want to suggest a critical skill—political mapping. Several of the leaders we interviewed talked about how important it was to map the power landscape early when entering a new leadership position, before one has begun to initiate any kind of change. Not only is it important to identify early on who are the formal decision makers, but it is important to find out who their influencers are and begin to understand who might serve as both the champions for and the opposition to equity-focused change. These key players may also be people that you want to connect with early in your tenure, involving them at key stages of your leadership entry process.

The typical questions are: Who are the people leading change inside and outside of the organization? Who are the formal decision makers? The influencers of the decision makers? Where might you find allies? Where might you find opposition? We suggest using the tool shown in table 3.3, adapted from the Harvard Graduate School of Education's Certificate in Advanced Education Leadership course on Driving Change. The organizational context and authorizing environment assessment can help you map the political landscape internally and externally in organizations.[22] In a later chapter, we will talk about how to use the information you have gathered to put a plan of action into motion.

FINAL REFLECTION

There is no question that context mattered greatly in all of our own personal experiences with leadership entry. Each time, we worked hard to understand both the organizational context and the social context, in relationship to our own personal and occupational contexts, relying on the strategies outlined in this chapter to surface implications for our entry. It was important for each of us to understand our charges clearly from the beginning, which influenced the way we thought about the design of our entry. We each built early relationships with key players to guide our thinking. And we invested in existing teams before disassembling them, so as not to lose their

TABLE 3.3 Mapping the landscape

QUESTIONS	ANSWERS (Be specific with actual names and titles)
• **Who is actively leading equity-focused change inside of your organization?** Which of these people might serve as partners or guiding team members during your entry?	
• **Who is actively leading equity-focused work outside of your organization and in the larger community?** Which of these people might serve as partners or guiding team members during your entry?	
• **Who are the decision makers in the organization?** Who might need to be won over to make equity-focused change possible? Which of these people might serve as partners or guiding team members during your entry process?	
• **Who are the influencers in and outside the organization?** (including the influencers of decision makers?) Note that these are people who may not have positional authority. Which of these people might serve as partners or guiding team members during your entry process?	
• **Who are the people or groups who are most likely to experience loss with equity-focused change?** Which of these people might serve as partners or guiding team members during your entry process?	
• **Who are the people or groups who will most likely actively oppose equity-focused change?** Of these people or groups, who is most likely to engage meaningfully in discussion? Which of these people might serve as partners or guiding team members during your entry process?	

Source: This tool was adapted from the "Organizational Context and Authorizing Environment Assessment" as featured in the Harvard Graduate School of Education's Certificate in Advanced Education Leadership course on Driving Change.

critical contextual insight. Understanding the context, with great humility and attention, was critical to our success as leaders.

If we could do it over again, however, there are a few things we would punctuate because of their importance. Each of us would have focused more on historical context, with an emphasis on talking not just to community leaders early on, but community elders, especially Asian, Black, Indigenous, and Latinx elders. We would have worked harder earlier on to understand the distribution of power. It was important to identify the voices that were most heard and why, so that we could later disrupt power hoarding. And we would have been more attuned from the beginning to the inevitable challenges of being deemed outsiders. The reality is that when you are an outsider, you don't always get straight information about the context. This makes the need for an advisory group or kitchen cabinet even more important. Insider or outsider, attention to context is essential for every leader.

As you plan for your leadership entry, consider these reflective questions:

- What do you know already about the organization you will be serving and the community in which it is situated?
- What do you know about the social and historical context? What else do you need to learn?
- What are the top-of-mind present-day challenges? How can you learn more about the social and historical context that surrounds them?
- Who can help you deepen your contextual understanding?
- How might your own personal and occupational context impact your leadership entry approach?

CHAPTER 4

BUILDING TRUST AND BEING TRANSPARENT

*The kindness of words creates trust, of thoughts it
creates depth, and of giving it creates love.*

—LAO TZU

The leaders we interviewed consistently shared how important it was to be transparent during their leadership entry. In other words, they believed it was critical to share their goals for entry up front and to communicate their planned actions, depicting them in well-defined phases like listening, sensemaking, communicating, and action planning. Leaders for equity did so, however, with a focus on building trust, especially trust across difference.[1]

Education researchers Anthony Bryk and Barbara Schneider describe *relational trust* as an essential ingredient for school improvement given the mutual dependencies that exist between principals, teachers, and parents.[2] Schools are complex ecosystems where each member's ability to do their job is connected to almost every other member. In other words, school communities only work when people can trust that everyone else is doing their part to serve students well. At the most basic level, consider the calculus teacher who depends on every previous math teacher to have prepared their students for the course. When a new leader joins an educational organization, everyone is wondering, can they be trusted? Meaning, can they depend on this leader to play their part in the organization and do it well? Building trust starts at the beginning.

According to Bryk and Schneider, building relational trust requires the discernment of respect, competence, personal regard, and integrity.[3] Leaders for equity understand that they cannot do the work alone, so building relational trust must be a fundamental objective of those early leadership actions. Here we share more about the discernment of relational trust along with some observations about the entry of new leaders in education organizations:

- *Respect.* Respect is demonstrated in the social discourse across a school community, especially in the act of listening.[4] A new leader must communicate with transparency from the start their intent to listen deeply to various perspectives, their commitment to weighing these perspectives before developing an action plan, and their process for doing so. The process of deep listening builds trust. For new leaders, know that your community will be asking themselves: Will the new leader listen to me?

- *Personal regard.* Personal regard is demonstrated when community members extend beyond the formal requirements of a job definition to show they care.[5] A new leader should not only share their intent to listen but share how and when they will do so. Outside of these formal opportunities to interact, the leader should be present, connecting with their community members in warm and welcoming ways that demonstrate their genuine care for others. Goodwill is accumulated when we get to know each other, too. For new leaders, know that your community will be asking themselves: Will the new leader go out of their way to see me and show they care?

- *Competence.* Competence is someone's ability to do the job that is expected of them.[6] New leaders must not only communicate their professional history and reasons for taking the job, but they will likely want to communicate with transparency their dual-track agenda. In other words, new leaders must do the job while learning about the organization simultaneously. When new leaders pay close attention to what they hear, while performing the fundamental aspects of the job to which they've been assigned, they can accomplish quick wins that will build trust and credibility. For new leaders, know that your community will be asking themselves: Will the new leader do their job well?

- *Integrity.* When someone lives by a set of values and acts on them, they demonstrate integrity.[7] For new leaders, it is critical to do more than just communicate their entry plan. They must follow through on it, report on what they learned, and put those lessons into practice through value-driven decision-making. This kind of follow-through makes them more predictable and trustworthy. For new leaders, know that your community will be asking themselves: Will the new leader keep their word?

What makes trust building more complex is that in education, we serve and support students, staff, and families who are members of a variety of racial and ethnic cultural groups, often different from our own or different from the White-dominant norm. Even when there aren't racial or ethnic cultural differences, an outsider to the organization will need to learn how to connect with the new organizational culture they have entered, which can be quite different. Entering a leadership role while centering equity requires leaders to engage with others through bicultural lenses to build trust across differences.[8] This requires understanding how culture operates at different levels of complexity. In her book *Culturally Responsive Teaching and the Brain*, Zaretta Hammond provides leaders for equity a pathway to understanding how to deepen trust by connecting at the cultural levels where transformational change can happen (see figure 4.1).[9]

Many leaders focus their efforts at building trust on connecting at the surface level of culture, which are those things that are readily observable. They make connections with people through food, music, and holidays. Making these cultural connections is important,

FIGURE 4.1 Zaretta Hammond's Culture Tree

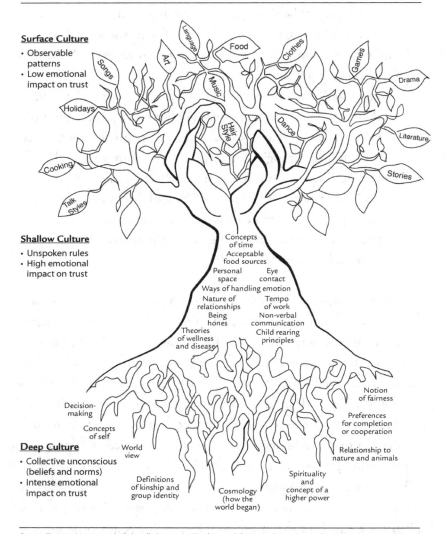

Surface Culture
- Observable patterns
- Low emotional impact on trust

Language · Food · Clothes · Games · Drama
Art · Songs · Music · Holidays · Hair Style · Dance · Literature
Cooking · Stories · Talk Styles

Shallow Culture
- Unspoken rules
- High emotional impact on trust

Concepts of time
Acceptable food sources
Personal space · Eye contact
Ways of handling emotion
Nature of relationships · Tempo of work
Being hones · Non-verbal communication
Theories of wellness and disease · Child rearing principles

Deep Culture
- Collective unconscious (beliefs and norms)
- Intense emotional impact on trust

Notion of fairness
Decision-making
Preferences for completion or cooperation
Concepts of self
World view
Relationship to nature and animals
Definitions of kinship and group identity
Spirituality and concept of a higher power
Cosmology (how the world began)

Source: Zaretta Hammond, *Culturally Responsive Teaching and the Brain: Promoting Authentic Engagement and Rigor Among Culturally and Linguistically Diverse Students* (Thousand Oaks, CA: Corwin, 2014).

but they are not enough to build trust. According to Hammond, leaders can build trust most effectively at the next level of culture, shallow culture, which she defines as a culture's invisible, unspoken rules. This level of culture includes how people handle emotion, their concepts of time, and how they work. Leaders who mirror and respect the practices of the community at this level of culture connect in highly emotional ways that build trust. Only then can a leader open the door to trust building at the deep cultural level, defined as a culture's values and beliefs, which include concepts of fairness and approaches to decision-making. Remaining attentive to all three levels of culture is important for leaders during entry as the levels are interdependent.

How leaders accomplish these tasks at a time in their leadership arc when they often have the least trust capital will be the focus of this chapter. In it, you will learn about Shin Tan, a leader of a school in Singapore who brought a community together through the forced merger of two schools.[10] He entered with transparency and built trust in a challenging context made even more difficult because he started months into the COVID-19 pandemic. Following Shin's story, we will explore facets of transparency and trust using his experiences as a guide, highlight a few key takeaways, and provide thoughts on some critical skills and questions to guide your entry planning. We hope you will come away with some ideas about trust building that you can put immediately into action.

TRUST AND TRANSPARENCY WHILE SOCIAL DISTANCING

When most leaders envision building trust as they enter a new role, they imagine making close connections through proximity. They hold one-on-one meetings and interviews. They bring people together over food. They roll up their sleeves and work alongside others. For Shin Tan, the vice principal of a newly merged high school in Singapore in the spring of 2020, however, the sudden challenges brought on by the COVID-19 pandemic would require new approaches to building trust.

That said, things were going to be challenging even before the pandemic hit. The school was created in January 2019, when two school communities merged due to enrollment changes. As a result, many things needed to happen well and quickly to ensure success, and understandably, there were hard feelings among some faculty members, given the many shifts in roles and reporting structures. While Shin was excited about supporting the merger, bringing his experience as a teacher and department head, he was cognizant that he was significantly younger than other vice principals in Singapore and younger than all the academic department heads who reported to him, which could exacerbate these hard feelings. He was also new to this school community, having spent the past year overseas, and he was starting his new role midyear.

Given the context, Shin knew he needed to be intentional about his leadership approach. First, he would address his youth with candor. It was vital for him to communicate what he did not know, express his value for his direct reports' experience levels early and often, and offer critical friendship, not expertise. He also knew he needed to respect the organization's culture, albeit an emerging one, taking time to learn about current ways of working before considering any changes. He appreciated how disruptive change might be, given that the school year was already in session and that he was an outsider. Humility and an orientation toward curiosity and learning would be essential. He also knew that his reserved nature would be a challenge in this environment. He would have to share something about it with his team to gain their understanding and support early on. He shared, "I don't think I am the most approachable person. My own students even told me that."

Shin assessed the tools for early relationship building at his disposal, given the social distancing restrictions, and he started small. He introduced himself to the school faculty through a welcoming email that outlined his goal of getting to know each staff member's motivations, aspirations, responsibilities, and challenges. Shin shared his guiding belief in growth mindset, commitment to excellence, and orientation toward building trusting relationships. He underscored these values by telling the story of a former student headed to law school despite being initially placed in a low achievement track. The email closed with an invitation to his direct reports to meet virtually with him one-on-one so that Shin could learn from each of them. In it, he also shared what questions he would ask (see "Shin Tan's Entry Interview Questions").

SHIN TAN'S ENTRY INTERVIEW QUESTIONS

- Please share a little about yourself, including what you'd like me to know about you.
- What do you think is your greatest strength that you bring to your job?
- Please share one moment at school in recent years (from 2018 to now) that you were most proud of.
- What do you find most frustrating about your job?
- Which area would you most like to grow in professionally?
- Are there specific groups of students for which you feel we have not done enough as a school?
- What is one thing (or more) I can do to help you do your job better?

Several opportunities to deepen trust surfaced during these initial interviews with his direct reports, all of them department heads. For example, one department chair had a strong desire to test programs that were in limbo due to the merging of the schools to determine whether they should continue in future years. Shin listened, could sense her passion, and found ways to advocate for her recommendation with the school principal. By championing her efforts, Shin not only strengthened his relationship with her but was instrumental in implementing a promising program. Later, he knew he could draw on that relationship to bring this department leader along on other efforts to move the school forward.

Through his initial interviews, Shin could also see opportunities to demonstrate his competency as a former math department chair.

For example, he learned that there were places where the curriculum could be more student-centered. Seeing an opportunity to contribute, Shin sampled several math assignments and evaluated their quality, looking for opportunities for improvement. Before sharing his observations with the current math department head, he checked in with other leaders to ensure his approach would not hurt the department head's feelings. Ultimately, the department chair received the feedback well and was able to make improvements quickly with Shin's support. Shin attributed this positive interaction to the character of the department chair and to the connection he built during their one-on-one interview.

When issues surfaced among the team, Shin sought out structural and environmental explanations instead of looking for fault in people. For example, based on observations he made during his initial interviews, he analyzed workload balance to ensure everyone was treated fairly. When Shin noticed an imbalance, instead of making assumptions, he talked to team members to identify root causes. He learned through these conversations that, for some, taking on additional projects outside of one's job description had been discouraged in the past. By empowering all team members to pursue additional projects when appropriate, these leaders started to operate at the same level as their peers. As he said wisely, "It takes two hands to clap." He took a similar approach to interpersonal conflict. When two of his direct reports showed up angry about a decision made at the school, Shin took them out to a socially distanced lunch. He knew that if he connected with them outside of the school building, he could attend to both the feelings surfacing in the outburst and the problem that caused the feelings. "Being out of the school can do wonders," Shin shared as he thought about this interaction. "It brings down people's guards so they can move forward."

Shin also noticed during his entry period that the teacher evaluation process felt like a "black box" for many educators. So he made the expectations clearer and broke down the process. These actions increased teacher confidence across the school, allowed for improved performance, and made performance evaluation more equitable, as teachers knew what actions would lead to each performance level.

Looking back on his first year as a vice principal managing a school merger during a global pandemic, Shin notes that trusting relationships were crucial to his successful entry into the role. He also reflects on what he could have done better. He wonders, for example, how he could have used these same practices with his students. As is likely not a surprise, Shin has already begun to take action on his insights.

OUR ANALYSIS

The relationship between trust, transparency, and improving outcomes in organizations is well documented. What is less understood is how leaders operate in the early stages of their role to build trust while relationships are still new. Using Shin's story as a through line, this section will examine how Shin demonstrated respect, personal regard, competence, and integrity, while bridging cultural differences.

Respect

What stands out in Shin's approach to entry is his commitment to listening to the perspectives of each member of his community. Through his entry interviews, Shin collected the views of those he led and created a space where each team member felt heard. In department meetings and emails, he shared themes from those interviews, so that his team knew what he was taking away. Even more, he distributed his attention differently based on need. He spent more time, for example, with those who felt marginalized by the school merger and made sure they knew that their perspectives and voices would help drive the improvement of the school. Actions that demonstrated respect not only reduced Shin's blind spots about the culture and climate of the school, but they also served to empower those he led. As a result, he could enact change aligned with his vision more quickly and with a greater chance for sustainability.

Personal Regard

Shin's approach to leadership entry was caring and human-centered. With all the meeting constraints that came with responding to the pandemic, Shin committed to frequently engaging with his colleagues in formal and informal settings. He met with people to see the organization and their role from their vantage point, rejecting the default narrative surrounding team members. Shin focused on their assets, defining the root causes of problems as primarily structural and not personal. He paid attention to fairness and threats to status. He made sure to ask how each person would feel about a particular change, thereby reducing anxiety and releasing that energy to reinvest in improvement efforts.

Competence

Shin was self-aware of the assets he brought to his new leadership role. His expertise in the math curriculum and student work analysis, for instance, allowed him to demonstrate how he could be helpful to the math department chair and build some credibility early on. However, demonstrating competence can be a tricky balancing act for leaders when working with direct reports with similar expertise. The leader can provide support, but must ensure that the person still has agency and isn't micromanaged. Shin's approach to supporting his math department chair reflected competence in the content area without stepping on toes. In doing so, he deepened his relationship with the department chair and increased trust in his leadership.

Integrity

Like most leaders who start with a formal entry process, Shin made his plan public. He gave everyone a bar by which to test whether he was a leader who kept his word. While many people would have likely given him a pass for falling short, due to the constraints of the pandemic, Shin was able to further build his reputation for credibility and integrity by delivering on the actions within his entry plan. He shared his values up front. The faculty and students could then determine the degree to which his actions reflected these values. And when he fell short, it allowed him to explain and adjust. The inevitable changes and course corrections in his entry process remind us that no one requires perfection from their leaders. Still, they want to have a sense of how their leader will communicate both changes and the rationale for those changes.

Building Trust Across Difference

Even those who share a common cultural identity with the communities they serve will have to build trust across differences. For Shin, his youth, newness to the community, and identity as someone returning from overseas were bridges he had to cross. All three levels of culture are addressed in Shin's interactions with his community. We see the connection to surface-level cultural differences in Shin's attention to communication preferences early on. When Shin met with teachers outside of the school building to discuss more emotionally charged topics, he demonstrated an initial understanding of and willingness to learn the unspoken rules and expectations of the school community, which opened the door for deeper trust. And for the team members marginalized by the merging of their two schools, Shin's attention to fairness and decision-making mirrored the community's core values and created space for connection at the deepest levels of culture. He further developed trust by making the promotion policy more transparent, recognizing teachers' needs for fairness. Shin demonstrated transparency in his practice and connected with people at all three levels of culture to create the conditions for trust rooted in high emotional impact.

IMPLICATIONS FOR LEADERS

Being transparent and building trust are critical ingredients for the success of a new leader. Even more, trust building can begin to change organizational culture in a positive way. If change is not happening in the way you would like, take time to reflect on the levels of culture. Here we draw out a few more specific ideas to guide you in the design of your leadership entry plan.

Share Your Core Values

When you introduce yourself to your new team, organization, or community, it is important to communicate your core values, including your explicit focus on equity and what that word means for you. If the organization already has value statements that align with your own, feel free to demonstrate that alignment. If it doesn't, you'll need to articulate your own. Either way, it is important for the people you work with and serve to know the principles that drive you. Core values, in our experience, are not just words on paper, but touchstones that help guide our decision-making, especially when faced with the toughest decisions and those where the answers are unclear. By expressing your commitment to equity from the start, and what that means for you, people will know where you stand and can hold you accountable to your word, which builds integrity.

Write a Formal Entry Plan and Communicate Your Progress

In addition to sharing who you are and what you stand for, we recommend creating and communicating a formal leadership entry plan and reporting on what you are learning along the way. Telling people what you are doing and why during those first few months on the job, and then following through on promises, will communicate respect, personal regard, competence, and integrity. It can also begin to build trust across difference when done with honesty. For a superintendent or CEO, this will likely mean producing a publicly accessible plan that articulates who you are, your goals for entry, your core values, and your entry activities. For a principal, it might mean sharing a similar plan with school community members like parents, staff members, community partners, and even students. For a department head at a central office, school, or nonprofit, this might look like a letter that you share with direct reports and the specific people your department serves. The plan can be a simple Word document or PowerPoint, translated into multiple languages depending on your context and supplemented with multimedia elements. A sample plan is given in the "Sample Entry Plan Outline" box on the next page.

From there, you'll want to keep people updated on both what you are doing and what you are learning. It is important not to assume that people read your initial entry plan, so following up and reinforcing your activities and their rationale is essential. Equity leaders ought to heed the advice of Kim Scott, the author of *Radical Candor*. She explains that the effectiveness of the message gets measured "at the listener's ear and not the speaker's mouth."[11] When communicating to large and diverse stakeholder groups, this means that trust is built by narrowing the message to the most essential content and sharing it multiple times using multiple modalities. Equity leaders go to people where they are and share information in the ways that are accessible. Whether it is through email, social media, phone calls, face-to-face meetings, or visiting door-to-door, what is important is that the leader chooses formats that privilege the preferences of their community rather than their own.

Do the Work and Participate as a Learner

During leadership entry, the leader must see the system and look for patterns, but they also need to build credibility by doing the work. While telling stories from your past work can help make connections, nothing is more potent than rolling up your sleeves and working alongside those you lead. Doing the core work of your

SAMPLE ENTRY PLAN OUTLINE

INTRODUCTORY LETTER
- Introduce yourself (consider a video introduction that hooks the audience into reading the rest of the plan)
- Include a picture, if appropriate
- Consider a callout box with the goals for your entry process

CORE VALUES STATEMENTS
- Describe why you are including them and how they drive the way you will enter into your new position

ACTION STEPS
- List the data you will gather
- List the people and groups you will talk with and how, including the questions you will ask
- List any other actions that may need to be addressed right away, depending on context

NEXT STEPS
- Share what you will do to make sense out of the data you gathered
- Share how you will communicate what you learned
- If appropriate, share your plan for taking what you learned into strategy development and action planning

CONCLUSION
- Thank everyone
- Share how they can get involved
- Share contact info, if appropriate

Note: This is an outline that Jen uses in her HGSE course on leadership entry, largely drawn from samples she has collected and studied. Many of these entry plans are reflective of the guidance provided by Barry Jentz in *Entry: How to Begin a Leadership Position Successfully* (Newton, MA: Leadership and Learning, 2012).

organization is the best way to understand it in depth, and there are few things as powerful for building trust as shared experience.

While leaning in to an area of expertise can be one way to build trust and create an early win, it can also be transformative to demonstrate your commitment to learning as a leader. Perhaps there is priority work already underway about which you know very little. For example, a school you are now leading may be in the middle of working on improving their use of formative assessment, or may be implementing new practices that support social-emotional learning. As a leader, you might incorporate these ideas into your own practice, whether in faculty or team meetings or by practicing alongside the teachers on your staff. When the leader learns with their team and publicly reinforces that learning requires making mistakes, trust builds across the organization.

Finally, doing the work is an excellent way to communicate the expectation that everyone in the organization must do whatever it takes to meet the needs of the organization's clients. That might involve the superintendent or CEO leading professional learning in an area of expertise or participating fully in professional education relevant to a critical organizational priority. This modeling can be compelling when a leader engages in tasks that are new or difficult. It reinforces the message that improving schools and districts requires risk-taking and that no one will be asked to do anything the leader isn't willing to do themselves.

Say Yes, and If You Have to Say No, Explain Why

When a new leader arrives, there is a natural inclination for employees to stop everything and ask permission to move forward. One of the most important moves a leader can make, one that builds trust, is to encourage team members and direct reports to continue doing their best work without microscopic supervision. Keep the trains running. You don't want to be a bottleneck to decision-making and progress before you've even gotten started. By resisting the temptation to do so, you will likely begin to change organizational culture positively from the start.

That said, there will be decisions you need to make early on. When you are new, big decisions can be especially difficult because you don't know what you don't know. One of the trickier moments in leadership entry is when you believe you know the right direction and the person responsible for the work thinks the exact opposite. Curiosity and reflective listening can often result in a shared or third path. When it doesn't, the leader will need to decide between their team member's perspective and their own. We suggest saying yes to the approach offered by the owner of the work, trusting that they know better, but make it time-bound so that you can evaluate its effectiveness. This allows the leader to communicate trust in those closest to the work, while giving yourself time to learn.

When new equity-focused leaders must say no due to resource constraints, safety, or other factors, it can be transformative to communicate what would need to be true to say yes. This kind of transparency about decision-making is critical to trust building. Imagine telling a direct report, "I can't support that assistant principal pipeline program now, because the cost per participant is much more than our other similar programs. However, if you can demonstrate how this program will help ensure the demographics of our building leaders mirror the demographics of our community and can reduce costs, I would reconsider my decision." Transparency around decision-making serves as a sign of respect and an opportunity to teach those you lead about how you think strategically or balance priorities.

A SKILL: TRUST GENERATORS

In her book, *Culturally Responsive Teaching and the Brain*, Zaretta Hammond summarizes five trust generators that help teachers build connection with students in the classroom.[12] In our experience, they are applicable for leaders, too, especially leaders who must build trust across differences. In table 4.1, we offer a set of considerations with attention to trust building for equity-focused leaders as they design their leadership entry plans.

TABLE 4.1 Entry Trust Generators

	ZARETTA HAMMOND'S TRUST GENERATORS	CONSIDERATIONS FOR THE DESIGN OF YOUR LEADERSHIP ENTRY
Proximity	People are more likely to build relationships with those whom they connect with across cultural levels. Engaging in what others value and mirroring their approach builds the connection on which the trust generators can begin.	As you design, consider: • How you will get close to the core work of your organization (e.g., through school visits or classroom observations) • How you will get close to the people who work in your organization (e.g., by walking the halls or eating lunch in the staff room) • How you will get close to the people you serve (e.g., by walking neighborhoods or taking public transportation) • How you will enter spaces where you might be an only or "other" of a salient identity with humility
Selective vulnerability	People respect and connect with others who share their own vulnerable moments. It means showing your imperfect human side.	As you design, consider: • How you might tell stories about yourself as a learner and about times when you struggled, and how those experiences inform your leadership • How you might talk about your experiences, successes, and failures working across differences, and how those experiences inform your leadership • How you will share what you are learning during your entry process for additional feedback • How you will own up to mistakes during your leadership entry and repair harm
Familiarity	People develop a sense of familiarity when they see someone often in a particular setting, such as at a bus stop every day or in the café on a regular basis.	As you design, consider: • How you will create predictable routines and stick with them (e.g., always have lunch in a school cafeteria or get coffee in the neighborhood where you know you'll run into people) • How you will post on social media or send communications in a predictable format • How you will consistently communicate updates on your entry and emerging themes
Similarity of interests	People create a bond with others who share similar likes, dislikes, hobbies, and so forth. This common affinity allows a point of connection beyond any obvious racial, class, or linguistic differences. This plants the seed of connection in the relationship.	As you design, consider: • How you will make personal connections (e.g., ask people about how they cultivate joy outside of work, or inquire about hobbies, family, and pets) • How to participate as a full member of your community and across communities (e.g., attend concerts, go to restaurants and movies, join a recreational sports club) • How to acknowledge and recognize local and national events and holidays that are significant to different groups within the community

continued

TABLE 4.1 *Continued*

	ZARETTA HAMMOND'S TRUST GENERATORS	CONSIDERATIONS FOR THE DESIGN OF YOUR LEADERSHIP ENTRY
Concern	People connect when others show concern for issues and events important to them, such as births, illnesses, or other life transitions. This plants the seed of personal regard.	As you design, consider: • How you will stay abreast of life and current events • How you will know to attend events that surface quickly in your community (e.g., demonstrations, memorials, vigils) • How you will recognize retirements or transitions that happen early in your entry before you fully build relationships
Competence	People tend to trust others who demonstrate they have the skill and knowledge, as well as the will, to help and support them. This plants the seed of confidence in others.	As you design, consider: • How you will share your entry plan and with whom • How you will track your promises and communicate when you deliver on them • How you will talk about race, gender, and sexual orientation and the impact of these topics on the work and on students, families, and staff. This includes demonstrating comfort with having candid conversations about race and privilege, especially if one is a White leader. • How you will name and interrupt patterns of inequity when you observe them during your entry process

Sources: Zaretta Hammond, *Culturally Responsive Teaching and the Brain: Promoting Authentic Engagement and Rigor Among Culturally and Linguistically Diverse Students* (Thousand Oaks, CA: Corwin, 2014); Karissa Thacker, *The Art of Authenticity: Tools to Become an Authentic Leader and Your Best Self* (Hoboken, NJ: John Wiley & Sons, 2016); *Culturally Responsive Leadership: A Framework For School & School System Leaders* (Long Island City, NY: Leadership Academy, 2020), https://www.leadershipacademy.org/wp-content/uploads/2020/09/Culturally-Responsive-Leadership-Actions-2020.pdf.

FINAL REFLECTION

In each of our experiences with leadership entry, we knew that being transparent and building trust would be critical to our success as new leaders, but it requires a degree of cognitive dissonance. When you are new, others will judge you based on mere minutes of interaction (or a little internet searching). And the disconnect between intent (how we want to be seen) and impact (how we are perceived) can be even greater when working across cultural differences. It can be hard on the heart and soul of a new leader not to be seen for who you are. Remember that building trust takes time and presence. In fact, it can be exhausting to be so present and using all your senses. But it is worth it, because working in this way will positively influence organizational culture far beyond those first months on the job.

As you plan for your leadership entry, consider these reflective questions:

- How will you communicate your entry plan to ensure transparency? How will you keep people updated on what you are doing and what you are learning along the way?
- How will you demonstrate respect, personal regard, competence, and integrity throughout your leadership entry process?
- What will you do to build trust across difference?

CHAPTER 5

LISTENING WITH EMPATHY

As leaders, we have no choice but to figure out how to invite in every-body who is going to be affected by change. Those that we fail to invite into the creation process will surely and always show up as resistors and saboteurs. But I haven't become insistent on participation just to avoid resistance or to get people to support my efforts. It's because no one person is smart enough to design anything for the whole system.

—MARGARET WHEATLEY, in *Finding Our Way*

In our empathy interviews with leaders, the importance of authentic listening arose as one of the most crucial leadership dispositions to take during the first months on the job. As one leader put it, "It is important because you don't know what you don't know, and it's dangerous to pretend you know things."[1] Once you have reflected on your own identity in relation to your organization's context, once you have scoped out and communicated a transparent process with attention to trust, it is time to put on your listening hat. But it isn't listening for the sake of it. A leader is listening to understand the way the organization works from the perspectives of both the people who work inside the organization and the people who belong to the community it serves.

But what do we mean by listening with *empathy*? According to Kathryn Pavlovich and Keiko Krahnke in their interdisciplinary exploration of the importance of empathy, it is "the capacity to experience and relate to the thoughts, emotions, and experience of others."[2] For new leaders, that means becoming cognitively and emotionally open to and aware of different perspectives on the organization's performance, reasons for that performance, and thoughts on how to address poor performance. This is not just an issue during entry; it is critical to establish an ongoing listening practice that will continue throughout a leader's tenure.

Listening with empathy, however, isn't something we just do. It takes emotional intelligence. Psychologist Daniel Goleman, who brought the concept of emotional intelligence to a broad audience, describes the underlying skills as follows (with some additional thoughts from us on the application to leadership entry):[3]

- *Self-awareness: The ability to recognize and understand your moods, emotions, and drives, as well as their effect on others.* In leadership entry, self-awareness is essential. As we've discussed previously, a new leader needs to be aware of their multiple identities because who we are influences how we see the world and how others perceive us. Self-awareness can also help new leaders avoid taking on more than they are capable of, overpromising and underdelivering, and pretending to know something they don't.
- *Self-regulation: The ability to control or redirect disruptive impulses and moods and the propensity to suspend judgment; the capacity to think before acting.* During leadership entry, it is essential to anticipate and be aware of emotional triggers. Leaders will inevitably hear painful stories or learn about points of view with which they adamantly disagree. This can be distressing and, for some, retraumatizing. Self-regulation does not mean that a leader can't show emotions, not at all, but they mustn't be prisoners to their emotions. Showing emotion is critical, but there is much a leader can do to minimize the possibility of being overwhelmed by emotions in a way that can cause harm.
- *Motivation: A passion to work for reasons that go beyond money or status and a propensity to pursue goals with energy and persistence.* If a leader's inspiration comes from money, a title, or

prestige, leadership entry will be challenging and motivation will be hard to sustain. New leaders need to communicate and demonstrate their authentic motivation for the organization to succeed and the community to thrive from the start.

- *Empathy: The ability to understand the emotional makeup of other people and skill in treating people according to their emotional reactions.* As we've already mentioned, empathy is critical in leadership entry. You want to see, understand, and explore multiple and conflicting versions of how the organization is functioning and why. Leading with empathy will often involve listening to stories that depict sadness, disappointment, anger, and loss. A new leader must listen with head and heart, always seeking understanding.
- *Social skill: Proficiency in managing relationships and building networks and an ability to find common ground and build rapport.* Leadership entry is all about building relationships, which requires tuning in to people and to the context in which your interactions take place. Socially attuned leaders know when it makes more sense to have an informal meeting over a formal one. They also pay close attention, read the room, and look for cues that tell them when to lighten the mood, slow down, change direction, or pause.

In addition to having the emotional intelligence necessary for deep listening, new leaders must intentionally seek out the voices of those who often don't get heard, with a focus on parents and students. Ann Ishimaru and her colleagues point out that our current engagement strategies constrain the role of nondominant families in schools who might otherwise be powerful partners.[4] As their report explains, these families often can't participate in traditional engagement sessions because of English-only communications, midday meetings, and bureaucratic procedures for registration. Beyond the structural challenges, however, these families are often fully aware that there are racialized (negative) assumptions at play, so they may choose not to engage as a form of resistance.

In other words, as much as listening is an obligation for effective leaders, the opportunity to listen is a privilege and is never guaranteed. New leaders must carefully seek out and structure opportunities for deep listening to various voices, with a focus on nondominant voices, to do the learning necessary to perform their jobs well.

In this chapter, we will highlight the leadership entry of Jason Kamras as he stepped into his role as superintendent in the Richmond (Virginia) Public Schools (RPS) in 2018.[5] His intentional approach to listening and learning prioritized the voices of the people most experiencing the problems the district faced. We will then analyze his work with a focus on emotional intelligence and engaging nondominant students and families. From there, we will offer some key takeaways about listening with empathy, offer some skills to practice, and then end with some reflective questions to guide leadership entry planning. Ultimately, we hope you'll come away with some solid ideas about listening to people with different viewpoints so that you can gain a deeper understanding of the issues that matter most.

DEEP LISTENING IN A NEW COMMUNITY

Jason Kamras admits he didn't know a lot about Richmond, Virginia, before applying for the job. Originally from New York, he had just spent twenty-two years in the District of Columbia Public Schools as an award-winning teacher (the US Teacher of the Year in 2005) and administrator, leading several high-priority projects alongside Chancellor Kaya Henderson. While Richmond was only 100 miles south of DC, he had never visited the community, only driven past the signs on I-95.

But he was coming to realize that he was ready to take on a superintendency, and he knew he couldn't lead just anywhere. He wanted to find a place where his combination of values, expertise, and lived and professional experience matched the needs of the community, and where he and his family could live. He believed that to lead well, you had to be a full participant in community life. Having heard that Richmond Public Schools was in search of a new leader, Kamras went on a day trip to learn more.

Just an hour and forty-five minutes away, he drove down, went to a restaurant, walked the streets, checked out a couple parks, and passed by a few schools. Throughout the day, he chatted with people, sharing that he was thinking of moving there and asking what they thought of Richmond. What he learned was that Richmond was a beautiful city, rich with diversity and filled with pride, but also grappling with the city's difficult past and ready to embrace a new future. After more reading, research, and deep consideration with his wife and family, he decided to put his hat into the ring.

Of course, once selected, he had a lot more learning to do. As he explains, "It's impossible to lead a community you know nothing about." Cognizant that he was a White man about to take on a major leadership role in the former capital of the Confederacy and in a school district that serves more than 90 percent youth of color, he needed to do his homework and plan his entry with intentionality. Before he even started, in addition to reading everything he could get his hands on, he pulled together a key group of advisers for a retreat to get their early perspectives. The group consisted of people who knew him before his life in Richmond along with new acquaintances well-connected in the Richmond community. He asked for their guidance on who to talk to—who were the people who had the most power and influence in Richmond, even without formal titles? Who could give him more insight into the community's painful history? Who could provide guidance on the school district's role in helping young people understand that history so that they could create a better future? Which voices needed to be centered and prioritized in the process? This group played a critical role in helping to shape his hundred-day entry plan, which he published shortly thereafter.

His final entry plan highlighted three core values—engagement, equity, and excellence—and in the engagement section of the plan, he wrote, "I believe that the work of public education must be done in collaboration with families and the community. That means going out of our way to listen to and learn from students, parents/caregivers, and the community at large." In alignment with this core value, he made a commitment to conducting over one hundred listening sessions in his first hundred days, spanning every part of the city and key constituent groups (see "Listening Session Schedule for the First Hundred Days").

In addition to what he put into his formal plan, Jason tried to make sure to attend all kinds of neighborhood and community

LISTENING SESSION SCHEDULE
FOR THE FIRST HUNDRED DAYS

- Visit every RPS school to meet with students, principals, teachers, and support staff
- Meet individually with each school board member to better understand the needs of each district
- Hold nine neighborhood town halls, one for each district, to meet with parents/caregivers and other community members[6]
- Hold five citywide town halls, one each for the faith, civil rights, nonprofit, higher education, and business communities
- Conduct twelve "living-room chats," three each for the East End, the West End, the Southside, and the Northside
- Meet with the mayor and his team, and each member of the city council
- Meet with each member of Richmond's Virginia Assembly delegation
- Launch "RPS Direct," a weekly communication directly from him to the public
- Launch four advisory cabinets, one each for high school students, parents/caregivers, teachers, and principals
- Hold a Twitter town hall

events, no matter how big or small, especially in marginalized communities. He distributed his contact information regularly and responded to every email he got, affirming issues and frustrations, and connecting people to team members who could address them. His take was that community members would never bother to come to events where he wanted feedback if they weren't sure if they really had a voice. His consistent response to these inquiries was critical.

And he would go anywhere he was invited. He said, "The Chamber of Commerce invites you for a cocktail hour and the Rotary Club for a talk, but it could also be a high school student, or a teacher, or a custodian who wants you to see the boiler." He also suggested that people call him by his first name to signal accessibility. As a White male educated at Princeton and Harvard, he needed to do everything he could to disrupt assumptions about his being disconnected and unrelatable. He said, "Simple, human connection opens up the doorway."

During each of these meetings, formal and informal, he would ask two simple questions: What do you really like about RPS/your children's school? What don't you like and what could be better? Keeping it simple was essential, as he has learned that "the gift of conversation is about the listening, not the asking." These questions seemed to open the door to a broad range of viewpoints about the district's past, present, and possible futures.

But when we asked Jason what he valued most, he unequivocally highlighted the living-room chats, which were arranged with support from his community engagement team. Designed to change the power dynamic so that parents and families might be more willing to share with him their real experience, it was one of the most important things he did. He still remembers his first chat with two Black mothers in one of the largest public housing complexes in Richmond, their children popping in and out of the conversation, depending on the topic. He listened intently that evening, only pausing to ask a member of the community engagement team who accompanied him to jot down action items when necessary. He just tried to be fully present and take in as much as possible.

All along, no matter the person or position, Jason was listening for initial patterns. What was popping up at the system level? What was popping up at the school level? How were the people who were most experiencing the problems describing them? What were the real issues at play? Each night, Jason would decompress and reflect on the themes that were beginning to emerge. While there were certainly different perspectives on the opportunities and challenges in Richmond, the initial emerging themes were clear and powerful.

For parents, the resounding issue was communication. He recalls that they said, "We don't know what is going on. We feel in the dark. We are not sure how to navigate things." Jason recognized through his deep conversations with them that parents and caregivers, especially those with language, economic, or cultural barriers, could not be effective partners if they weren't getting good information about what their children were learning, how they were learning, and the progress they were making, and they wanted it desperately. As a result, Jason talked to his team and set a new standard for excellent communication. He shared half-jokingly, "I wanted parents to be annoyed by the number of texts, emails, and phone calls they are getting from us. Then we would know we had met the mark." Jason realized that effective communication was a necessary condition for excellent teaching and learning.

For students, the loudest theme was about the quality of school facilities. Again, he understood from his ongoing dialogue with them that it was difficult for students to do their best work when basic facilities were not functioning, like the bathrooms. He can still remember a meeting on the Southside of Richmond, a primarily Latinx community, where one parent expressed, in tears, how she and her family felt about the poor conditions of the school facility. And while he felt overwhelmed in that moment by all that needed to be done, the deferred maintenance that had piled up over the years, he left knowing that he would attack the issue head on with an initial focus on the disrepair in bathrooms, which were of critical importance to the students he served. For them, this was much more than a facilities issue. The lack of functioning bathrooms stood in the way of their ability to learn and thrive in school.

And in talking with community and city leaders across racial and economic lines, he learned that there was a lack of trust in the district's ability to use its resources well. There was a general sense that money was not the problem and that funneling more money into the district was a mistake. He held a town hall on the subject to open more dialogue and to increase transparency about the district's budgeting process. He realized through his dialogue with community members that lack of trust in the school district would be a barrier to the district's long-term success, and the only way to build trust was to bring people together.

The initial emerging themes presented opportunities for initial action, but they also presented openings for larger, strategic conversations. Framing these listening sessions and the themes that emerged as initial steps in a larger process of identifying and winnowing strategic priorities was critical. Ultimately, Jason fell in love with the Richmond community through his deep engagement with them. This is the community he was meant to serve. And his ongoing motivation to listen was aimed at cultivating the shared understanding necessary to do so.

OUR ANALYSIS

There is so much to learn from Jason Kamras's entry into RPS. In this section, we delve deeper into his demonstration of emotional intelligence as well as some of his thinking about engaging marginalized groups. In each section of our analysis, we will incorporate additional details that demonstrate how Jason positioned himself to listen with empathy during his first months in the Richmond community.[7]

Self-Awareness

Jason's awareness of himself certainly influenced the way he showed up for these listening sessions. As a White man coming from the DC Public Schools, which has a reputation for big-city reform, and with an Ivy League pedigree, he chose to drop the title, the entourage, and the formality. While this wouldn't be the right move for every leader, depending on their identities and the context, it was important for him to present himself as approachable, responsive, and connected. As he explained in our interview, he didn't want people to perceive him as just another school district bureaucrat, but as a teacher who cared deeply about children and their families. During his school visits, for example, he never had an entourage and always made sure to reserve time to talk with teachers, visit classrooms, and chat with front office staff, custodians, and food-service workers.

Self-Regulation

Jason also understands that listening is a skill, one that he has honed over time. He shared that in DC, he could remember feeling the impulse to interrupt, correct, explain, or defend during difficult meetings. It was watching former chancellor Kaya Henderson in action that taught him what it looked like to listen, to acknowledge challenges, to probe for understanding, without jumping to problem-solving. Regulating our need to fix problems through simplification is critical. Each of the themes that Jason surfaced in his first hundred days, for example—communications, facilities, and budget—risks oversimplification. Jason used the process, however, to get underneath and behind the issues to examine their complexity, knowing that they were entry points into larger, more strategic conversations, and not just technical challenges that needed to be fixed.

Motivation

While Jason had a robust leadership entry plan, we want to emphasize all that he did beyond the formal plan. He shared his contact information widely, responded to emails in a timely manner, and met regularly with employees or community members at their request. He shared with us his view that if someone took the time to write their concerns down or to request the meeting, then it must be important. Jason treats every meeting as valuable, every person worthy of his time, and every exchange, even with those who are critical of his leadership, as a bid for attention.

Empathy

While the questions that leaders ask are meant to solicit advice from their community about what to hold on to, what to shed, and what to build, the information they receive will often come in the shape of stories. Embedded within are the answers to our questions. It is critical for a leader to embrace these stories, to use them to step into another's shoes, and to take clues from them about how the organization is currently working. But listening to stories can be exhausting. Taking time to decompress regularly, as Jason described, is critical.

Social Skill

Jason has a very calm, focused energy. He asks good questions and provides thoughtful answers. He has a way of making everyone feel important and valued. And he is extremely humble. One critical decision we wanted to note was that Jason decided not to take notes during his listening sessions and instead assigned a staff member to take notes only on time-sensitive action items. That put the onus on him to process information and identify emerging themes after each meeting. While he carried the burden of this additional processing time, he wanted to be fully present and put people at ease during the sessions.

Marginalized Voices

Finally, and most importantly, Jason went out of his way, as demonstrated by his living-room chats, to listen to people who might not otherwise be heard. He structured these meetings around the schedules of parents, in their own homes, and provided interpretation when necessary. But one of the most important nuances that Jason shared was about the importance of invitation. While an invitation from the superintendent might mean a lot for some folks, his receiving an invitation was often more important. His advisory group, as well as his community engagement team, served as critical liaisons into spaces he might not otherwise be able to enter, like the living rooms of parents who hadn't been served well by the system in the past.

We also recognize the small things that Jason does to express his respect for the community he serves, especially those from nondominant groups. He always thanks people for their feedback, even when it is difficult to hear, and holds himself accountable for staying true to his word. For example, he shared with us that when he meets a parent while out at a community or neighborhood event who has reached out to him, he checks in with them, "Did I respond to you? Did I follow through?" He knows that trust will grow only if he listens.

IMPLICATIONS FOR LEADERS

In addition to thinking about emotional intelligence and the importance of centering marginalized voices while listening, we wanted to draw out a few actionable implications for the design of your equity-focused leadership entry plan that will help set up your listening sessions for success.

Ask the Right Questions

It is critical to decide on a few broad questions that you plan to ask everyone up front, and to share them in advance. Depending on the group, these questions can be modified and supplemented with probing questions, but asking a few common, meaty questions across groups will help you draw out themes later. As one of our interviewees shared during our empathy interviews, "What are the three questions you'll ask everybody?"[8]

In our experience, a good starting point is to ask a question about strengths, a question about challenges, and a question about opportunities. The key is to write big, open-ended questions.

- What are the organization's most significant strengths? What would you want to see unchanged or amplified? Why?
- What are the organization's most significant challenges? What would you want to see changed or discontinued? Why?
- What are the ripest opportunities for progress? What would you want to see the organization start doing immediately, a year from now, three years from now? Why?

Barry Jentz and Jerome Murphy, in their 2005 article on leadership entry, suggest questions that fall into four categories:[9]

- *What* questions (What do stakeholders think the organization should be doing?)
- *How* questions (How does the organization really work?)
- *People* questions (What do people care about?)
- *Leadership* questions (What do people expect of the new leader?)

Another powerful approach to consider is the process of Appreciative Inquiry (AI), which takes a more asset-based approach to the development of questions and the structure of the dialogue.[10] AI is a process by which community members envision possible futures and together construct ways to bring those futures to life. Once the focus on the process is identified, participants offer answers to aspirational questions, like "What gives life?" and "What might be?", before entering into a process of constructing strategies using questions like "What should be?" It is important to note that there is fair criticism of AI's potential to squelch meaningful conversations about problems. However, if done thoughtfully, we believe questions formulated with an AI framework in mind can help generate more robust visions of what is possible before tackling the challenges and problems that stand in the way and constructing solutions.

Center Nondominant Voices

With a good set of core questions, leaders must then ensure that they gather a broad and well-rounded set of perspectives on the answers to those questions. No one should be excluded or overlooked, but conversations can be prioritized and staged. In our experience, prioritizing conversations with those who deliver and receive our organization's services earlier in the process can help the leader ask better probing questions of those who play supporting roles later. Education leaders need to listen first and foremost to broad swaths of students, school-based staff, and parents with various lived experiences and representing a variety of demographic groups. Leaders need to listen to their bosses, their colleagues, and their direct reports. They also need to listen to key players, like union leaders, elected officials, and community leaders.

But that isn't enough. Equity-focused leaders must seek special insight from those most experiencing the problems. Leaders of education organizations must center the voices of Asian, Black, Indigenous, and Latinx youth, staff, and families. They must seek out the voices of immigrant families, lift the voices of LGBTQ+ youth, court-involved youth, and homeless youth, and center the perspectives of students, family members, and staff with disabilities. Leaders will also want to think about often marginalized employee groups. Those roles might include special education assistants, security assistants, and food service providers in schools and school districts. The dedicated people who perform these roles have incredible insight into the daily functioning of the organization and the people it serves. Finally, we have learned the critical importance of listening to community elders. Listening to past racial and social justice leaders, for example, is crucial so that leaders can learn what was done before, the progress that was made, the challenges that arose, and identify the implications for the work of today. Each organizational context is different, but seeking out the perspectives of those pushed to the margins of our communities is critical in every scenario.

Doing so, however, will take intentionality and attention to trust building. We cannot emphasize enough how important it is to carefully structure focus group meetings with nondominant community members, even if the leader shares some of their life experiences. For example, these meetings might need to be brokered by a trusted community member; facilitated by a trusted and experienced facilitator, perhaps one chosen by the group; and less structured than larger and broader group sessions. It may also take several meetings before the group can talk freely about their greatest hopes, worries, challenges, and ideas for positive change. We also suggest building relationships in more informal settings and with no agenda, like at school and community events or over coffee or lunch, which can help set the stage for deeper conversations about problems and opportunities.

Listen with Curiosity and Begin to Pay Attention to Patterns

The process of listening to a variety of voices will inevitably surface conflicting points of view. And the answers will come in many shapes and sizes, including in the form of stories. The key is to listen with curiosity and to begin to pay attention to patterns. One framework that is useful for noticing emerging patterns is the Seven Circle model, developed by Steve Zuieback and Tim Dalmau, based on the work of Margaret Wheatley, and adapted by the National Equity Project (see figure 5.1).[11] The mode represents the components of an organization or living system. The components above the green line represent the technical aspects of the organization to which leaders often pay more attention. The components below the line represent the relational aspects of the organization, which are too often

FIGURE 5.1 National Equity Project's Seven Circle Model

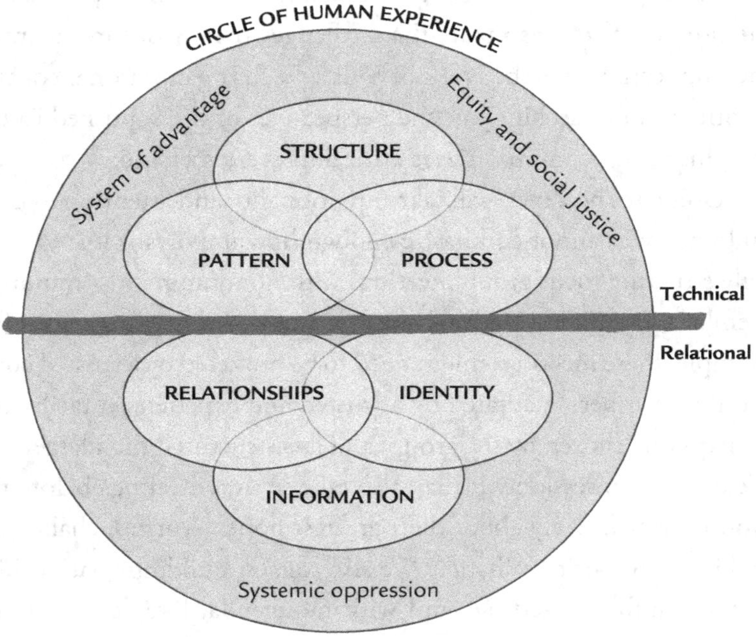

CIRCLE OF HUMAN EXPERIENCE

System of advantage

Equity and social justice

STRUCTURE

PATTERN   PROCESS

Technical

Relational

RELATIONSHIPS   IDENTITY

INFORMATION

Systemic oppression

Source: Adapted from the Dalmau Network Group www.dalmau.com.

overlooked. In this version of the model, the organization is situated within a larger circle of human experience of advantage and oppression, as well as equity and social justice.

As you listen with empathy, you may notice patterns:

- Patterns related to the systems, structures, and routines that define how things work in the organization
- Patterns related to trust, information flow, or how people talk about the organization and one another
- Patterns that demonstrate how power is distributed

We also suggest that the leader keep track of quick wins and specific action items. In addition to larger patterns and trends that will flow into sensemaking and action planning, there will inevitably be things that the leader wants to address immediately.

A SKILL: MINDFUL LISTENING

We also note that listening with empathy can be depleting, especially when what you hear is retraumatizing, which brings us to our last point. According to psychologist Adam Waytz, empathy is not only exhausting, but it has its limits (meaning, the more empathy you give to your community, the less you may have for your family), and it can exacerbate existing biases if not balanced.[12] So when you structure your listening sessions, take care of yourself. Don't schedule challenging listening sessions back-to-back. You likely can't let someone else take your place, but you can bring more colleagues into the process to share the responsibility. Consider involving others who can listen alongside you. And go for balance.

One particular strategy that we think is helpful is what Shane Safir calls "mindful listening." She says, "Applying mindfulness to our listening will help us create healthy below-the-green-line conditions and gather pertinent above-the-green-line data. By slowing down to observe the present moment—our breath, our autopilot thoughts and feelings, and other people's dispositions—we multiply the options available to us."[13] Table 5.1 shows Safir's Mindful Listening tool modified for use during leadership entry.[14]

FINAL REFLECTION

In each of our experiences with leadership entry, we learned that human connection was what mattered most. We learned that if we got to know people, and people knew us in return, they would rally for us, keep us out of trouble, and help us make things happen. In other words, through deep listening and by modeling vulnerability, people could see that they were cared about, and they cared in return.

TABLE 5.1 Shane Safir's Mindful Listening tool

Use this tool to prepare for your listening sessions and to debrief afterward.

STEPS	NOTES AND REFLECTIONS
1. **Self-awareness.** Before the session, look into the mirror: • Who am I in this listening session through the lenses of race, culture, gender, age, and role? • What unconscious biases may be at work in my brain? • What messages might I be conveying, consciously or not? • What am I listening for?	
2. **Other awareness.** Stand in the other's shoes: • Who is the person/are the people in this listening session through the lenses of race, culture, gender, age, and role? • What unconscious biases may be at work in their brains? • What does the person/group seem to care about most in this listening session? • What are they listening for?	
Given all of this, how would you like to show up?	
3. **System awareness.** Look back on how the session went by stepping up on the balcony to analyze the various forces at play: • How would you describe the listening session? • What nonverbal behaviors stood out to you? • What indicators of trust did you see? Was there evidence of rapport, genuine listening, and mutual regard? • How were issues of identity, power, or bias at play? • Did the interaction reflect other patterns in the system? • What structural factors could be influencing it (e.g., time, place, protocol)?	
What are you learning that will have implications for future sessions? For follow-up items?	

Source: We reprinted, with permission, the Mindful Listening tool with slight modifications. The original tool can be found in its entirety in Shane Safir, *The Listening Leader: Creating the Conditions for Equitable School Transformation* (San Francisco: Jossey-Bass, 2017), and a printable version can be requested on Safir's website, shanesafir.com /resources.

Empathic listening is a critical leadership stance that will not only serve you well during leadership entry, but throughout your tenure as a leader.

As you plan for your leadership entry, consider these reflective questions:

- Who do you need to talk to? And how can you gain multiple perspectives?
- How will you gain access to nondominant voices, especially parents and students?
- How will you prepare yourself to be fully present? How will you show up?
- What questions will you ask? And what will you listen for?
- What routines will you use to reflect and decompress afterward?

CHAPTER 6

CULTIVATING UNDERSTANDING

I think that the thing I most want you to remember is that research is a ceremony. And so is life. Everything that we do shares in the ongoing creation of our universe.

—SHAWN WILSON

Once a new leader has collected various data to inform their understanding of the organization, including qualitative data gathered during their initial round of listening, it is time to pause and make sense of the information collected. However, equity-focused leaders have a responsibility to perform their data analysis with love and care for the community they serve. While analysis of a variety of performance indicators and summative results is essential, building compassionate understanding requires interpreting that data with attention to the desires, needs, and experiences of the people behind the numbers.

One's approach to data analysis is vital because the way we present, analyze, and interpret data can dangerously oversimplify the issues and lead to faulty or harmful solutions. When we repeatedly perform simple comparative data analyses that focus on racial achievement gaps, for instance, reinforcing White achievement as the standard of excellence, we reinforce stereotypes and choose solutions that don't get at the real problems, needs, or aspirations of the students we serve. We want our data analysis to result in a kind of consciousness, a nuanced and deep understanding, that leads us to solutions to the real problems our organizations and communities face.

Ivory Toldson, professor of counseling psychology at Howard University, talks about the importance of using good data and thoughtful analysis to produce a compassionate understanding that dismantles harmful stereotypical myths about Black students.[1] His framework, we believe, can be beneficial for new educational leaders as they analyze the data collected during their entry periods in responsible ways:

- *Good data.* "Good data is comprehensive, holistic, and provides a complete picture of important issues."[2] As a new leader, it is crucial to make sure you've gathered a range of quantitative and qualitative information that lends itself to a complete picture or story about the organization. Too many people carry around in their heads what Toldson calls "bad stats"—statistics, often with unknown or unreliable origins, that they have heard and repeated and taken as common knowledge. These statistics often lead to assumptions about the performance and possible futures of the people we serve, especially students and families of color. For new leaders analyzing the data from leadership entry, the "good stats" data might include student achievement data, information about access to opportunity, and survey results about perceptions of the organization, in addition to the data gathered from one's listening sessions.

- *Thoughtful analysis.* "A thoughtful analysis requires a subjective connection to the data."[3] Once a wide range of data is collected, it is critical to disaggregate the data into demographic groups, but the analysis cannot stop there. Toldson suggests several analytic strategies that can lead to more meaningful conclusions, including within-group analysis, the analysis of growth data, and analysis across intersecting groups, like disability, language, gender, or socioeconomic status. Within-group analysis of students performing at different achievement levels, using multiple quantitative and qualitative data sources, for example, can help identify the specific factors that may inhibit or drive success for a particular group of students. For new leaders conducting leadership entry, the leader's inquiry questions must guide data analysis. What is it the leader is trying to understand? Well-crafted inquiry questions will help the leader determine what kinds of analyses to conduct with which sets of data, including what additional data the leader should collect or request.

- *Compassionate understanding.* "Lack of compassion is rooted in explicit and implicit biases."[4] Our data analysis processes must provide an opportunity to confront the biases that might cloud our judgment or lead to pathologizing students of color. Instead, educators must interrogate the data, ask questions about its origins, contextualize it, look for nuance, and test assumptions. As Toldson explains, this is the common courtesy that Black students, and all students, deserve when we believe in them. For leaders to make sense of the data they gathered during leadership entry, it is critical to surround yourself with people who will check your biases and bring multiple perspectives, including participants represented in the data reviewed.

In this chapter, we'll share the story of David Herrera as he entered his role as executive director of the Office of Equity for the Federal Way (Washington state) Public Schools, with an emphasis on sensemaking and data use.[5] We'll then analyze his approach using Toldson's framework: good data, thoughtful analysis, and compassionate understanding. From there, we will share a few implications for leadership entry and offer a skill to practice with the goal of helping new leaders gather, analyze, and interpret data in humanizing ways that are rooted in love.

DATA USE FROM THE GROUND UP

A few months into the COVID-19 pandemic, the Federal Way Public Schools, a district serving primarily students of color just outside of Tacoma, Washington, needed a new leader for their equity office after experiencing a change in leadership each year since the office began five years earlier. David Herrera, who identifies as Latino and Jewish, started his new role as the office's executive director in June of 2020.

The district hired David to bring cohesion to equity and anti-racist practices across district departments while also leading his own department, which offers a wide array of services: Native education, homeless and foster care supports, truancy, school safety, social-emotional learning, positive behavioral interventions and supports (PBIS), discipline, and athletics. While excited about the role, he could see that the roles in the department assigned to him were a hodge-podge mix, and had been given the "equity" label based on a set of assumptions that he would have to examine. He was also aware that equity offices are often established for symbolic reasons alone and that he would have to work especially hard to clarify the office's purpose.

To successfully enter this role, he would need to gain access to a comprehensive collection of data, begin to surface questions about the data, cultivate his new team so that they could help him make sense of the data, and gain understanding quickly, because there was pressure to create positive change across the school system during a challenging time. When David presented his entry plan to the school district cabinet for feedback, he asked that he immediately gain access to the district's data and information systems to explore them in his first thirty days. It was hard to know what questions to ask without an initial review of the available information.

From there, he started conversations with his new set of direct reports, mostly listening for team dynamics—with a particular focus on threats to their ability to collaborate. What came through in these conversations was how disconnected the new team felt. This dynamic was certainly something he would need to address, but he had to dig deeper to do so with precision. He wondered, for example, what connections might already exist below the surface on which he could build. David drew a team map to see who was connected to whom through previous work, friendships, and history, and existing relationships emerged. Through conversation and observation, it also became clear that some team members from non-dominant social groups or lower status roles worked in more acute isolation from the rest. He used this information to identify opportunities for collaboration and pair people purposefully on projects currently underway—building connections where they did not exist.

As people began working together, David then wanted to make the reasons for their collaboration clear. For example, he wanted everyone on the team to understand each other's contributions. He started a virtual document where each team member could share their successes, celebrations, key issues, and priorities for the upcoming week. In the beginning, David would review these updates and connect three or four people with similar challenges or priorities via email. But over time, the group began to study the document themselves and make their own connections and suggestions. Their common purpose began to emerge.

David built additional commitment to collaboration by putting in place a process for developing shared goals and metrics that were important across the diverse functions in the department. He had each individual review the district strategic plan and identify all the key metrics that they felt had a personal connection to their roles. The team then prioritized these metrics, with an eye towards identifying those that were most meaningful. Despite very different titles, roles, and responsibilities, the team coalesced around two main focuses: scholar participation in class and the percentage of students who feel their school is safe and welcoming. This helped the group to see themselves as a team with a common purpose.

With more vigorous collaboration habits and an increasing sense of common purpose, David began using data to build a shared understanding of the problems they might collectively try to solve. However, before he could get started, he first needed to know what his team members valued about data and data uses. At each department meeting, David decided to ask two people to colead a fifty-minute session on what data they paid most attention to and how they came to see it as necessary. The "Data Empathy Protocol" box describes the process David used to support team members with this task. For the first session, he intentionally asked two leaders of color who did not have powerful titles to share their perspectives. These leaders spoke

DATA EMPATHY PROTOCOL

Share with your team that you want to learn more about the organization, department, or team from their perspectives. Tell them that you are creating pairs responsible for sharing data at the next few staff meetings. Each pair will have fifty minutes to present their answers to the following questions:

In your role,

- What data are you paying attention to?
- How did you come to see it as important?
- What does it currently tell you about your work and priorities?

The pairs can present together or divide the time however they feel is appropriate. They can create tasks and materials for sharing information, sensemaking, discussion, and action. Both what they share and how they share it is data for your leadership.

NOTES FOR THE FACILITATOR:

As teams present, consider the data sources they select. What are you learning about what matters to them based on the sources they choose, how they present it, and the degree to which they work together? What patterns do you see in data selection? Where might there be agreement or tension?

When selecting the order, consider how you can use this activity to disrupt patterns of power. Are there team members who are closest to the work who aren't typically listened to in meetings? Are there team members with nondominant identities whom the group or organization marginalizes?

When determining pairings, consider putting people together who do not usually work together so that you can start to build relationships and empathy through the task.

to their data and did so by sharing their stories. Each team member spoke to their connection to the community and how it mattered for their work. When reflecting on the presentation, David shared that "this message of humanizing data, of constructing shared meaning grounded in story and relationship was so powerful." It was an incredible experience for the team that provided insight into new ways of thinking about gathering qualitative data through stories, especially stories that depicted the real experiences of the students they served. It also broke through the narrative that any collaboration among the department members could only be perfunctory—the team learned that they could work together, and that collaboration could be meaningful to each member both in their work and personally.

With knowledge that the problems that they wanted to solve would need to be addressed together with the people closest to them, David started joining his team in their work in schools and the community. He participated in their meetings with community partners, for example, so that he could better understand how outside organizations viewed the district and the equity office. David also asked these organizations where he could go to best learn about the needs, concerns, and desires of the new community he served.

With this new wealth of ideas about data sources and data use in hand, they practiced putting the data to work. For example, there were twenty-three family liaisons within the district, a group that David described as "the deepest holders of knowledge about what kids and families need," and his team sensed they were overworked. After an initial review of the data, they had a hunch about the root cause that they wanted to test. So he asked the family liaisons to do something simple—tally the requests they received from teachers to contact families and note whether the teacher tried themselves before asking for help. The team disaggregated this data by school and found consistent patterns. They then presented this information, coupled with observations made by the family liaisons, to the superintendent along with recommendations for how to support teachers in building relationships with families. The superintendent adopted this new approach and role for family liaisons. It was exciting to see that their strategic use of data, driven by authentic inquiry questions, could produce change.

While exploring and using various data within his department, David also started observing how data was used in other departments. Like many school districts, he found that the conversations were deficit based, primarily focused on performance gaps between Black and White students on state standardized assessments. Understanding that in his new role he was in a position to support and influence departments outside of his own, David invited the director of assessment to a session at the University of Washington focused on humanizing data. This opportunity to learn together about new ways of using data offered him an entry point for future collaboration around data use districtwide.

A year later, David's team is cohesive, clear on its purpose, and making a positive impact. He is collaborating with colleagues to change how the district uses data beyond his team and in partnership with community. He wants district teams to learn to use data to understand their most intractable equity-focused problems in areas such as staff diversity and student discipline. But David also wants to push the narrative about data use. In particular, he is trying to change the perception that districts can't move quickly by encouraging his colleagues to gather data, make sense of it, try things, and communicate changes in more rapid cycles. For him, data is only valuable when it can support people in cultivating the deep understanding that sparks action, creating the momentum for positive change.

OUR ANALYSIS

There is much to be learned from David Herrera's story of leadership entry, focusing on data use and collaborative sensemaking. In this section, we'll look at how David leveraged the use of holistic data through thoughtful analysis to create compassionate understanding, drawing out some of the nuances of his approach.

Good Data

David clearly understood the importance of balancing quantitative and qualitative data to get a more well-rounded understanding of the equity-focused challenges he faced. Every one of these challenges, he knew, was much more complex than it seemed on the surface. His decision to use the data empathy protocol, however, was a powerful way to surface new ways of thinking about data collection and its use collaboratively. By doing so, he and his team members could expand their thinking beyond the typical data stored in information systems. They were able to learn about one another and the valuable information and insight they could bring to problem-solving. But most importantly, they were able to identify data that were seen as "good" and, therefore, more likely to inspire change in practice. So often, we look at data that does not provide insight or questions worth pursuing. Getting consensus up front on data sources that are meaningful was a decisive early leadership move.

Thoughtful Analysis

To understand the issues better, David knew he would need a team that could help him make sense of this more holistic set of data through their collaborative analysis. But they couldn't do that until they could bond, see each other's strengths, learn to ask questions together, and engage in dialogue. To better understand team dynamics, he utilized David Rock's SCARF Threat model to identify and examine the concerns that were standing in the way of the new team's ability to collaborate.[6] Specifically, he listened for threats to status, certainty, autonomy, relatedness, and fairness to understand what experiences triggered pain or frustration at work. But rather than act on the surface observation that emerged from these initial interviews—that the team felt disconnected—he decided to dig deeper, gather more nuanced information, and create a map of existing connections to build from strengths and more precisely address the issues. Doing so allowed him to cultivate a sense of team connectedness essential for them to engage in the thoughtful analysis and discourse required for their success. David understood that he couldn't just dive into data analysis with his team without building their mutual trust and capacity to work together.

Compassionate Understanding

With a more comprehensive set of data and stronger relationships on the team, they were able to pursue deeper understanding of the problems that they collaboratively identified, a level of understanding that led to action. For example, the team identified the problem of family liaisons being overworked and made sure to include the family liaisons themselves in the sensemaking process because they knew the wealth of knowledge they had to share. Together, they collected additional data to test their theories, and ultimately, they were able to make a successful recommendation to the superintendent. David's success working with his team also laid the foundation for him to begin working credibly with teams across the organization, positioning him to disrupt the deficit thinking that dominated many data-driven conversations and to elevate the voices of the people represented in the data.

IMPLICATIONS FOR LEADERS

Building compassionate understanding is essential if we are to communicate with authenticity about strengths, challenges, and opportunities and galvanize our communities for action. However, the sensemaking process during leadership entry is too often done *to* our organizations and communities and not *with* them, as if we are the experts or saviors. This kind of isolated sensemaking can not only result in surface-level understanding and misdiagnosis of the current state, but it may produce harm and alienate those we serve. Here we'll highlight a few actionable implications that can support new leaders in identifying and interpreting the data they've collected during entry to gain a fuller understanding.

Bring People In

To be clear, we believe that sensemaking should be happening at every stage of the leadership entry process in partnership with the community. As in David Herrera's example, sensemaking is iterative, emerging through hundreds of interactions in collaboration with others over time. But after a leader has spent time listening, there is a more formal pause that must occur. The leader must review the data gathered holistically, test assumptions, and grasp the insights and implications for the future. At this stage, we suggest that a new leader put together a team (or a portfolio of teams or advisory groups) to help them make sense. At the very least, this group should include one's leadership team or direct reports, but an equity-focused leader should also invite participants more proximate to the work they lead, like teachers, parents, and students. All team members, including youth, should be seen as essential partners who share necessary experience and knowledge. This inclusivity allows for liberatory collaboration, where leaders are making meaning alongside the community they serve.

As important as the composition of the team is the kind of environment that is created. For deep sensemaking to occur, we would suggest longer periods of time in which to work. Ideally, this would be a retreat for a day or two—with food provided—where members can dedicate their full time to discussion. Depending on the time demands of your participants, it could be spaced out over a more extended period, but still allow for half-day sessions to ensure the breathing room needed to process. Ongoing processing can happen in shorter chunks, but the initial sensemaking during leadership entry requires time dedication.

Ultimately, this sensemaking venue should function as a "holding environment," defined by psychologist Robert Kegan as a space that can assist people in the often painful growth process.[7] We realize that this sets a high bar for the sensemaking environment, but interpreting our surroundings is one of the most important things we do as leaders. That is because data analysis is not just about the subject at hand, but about our personal reflection and growth, testing our frames of reference and the assumptions we often make. Participants should be able to share their points of view, ask questions, disagree, and reflect. The leader should not have to be protective, political, or polished. The container you create should allow everyone to acknowledge current understandings and push themselves and each other in new ways that will change how they view the work. If done well, the team's sensemaking routines will influence how they understand and function in the world. And many leaders will hold onto these advisory groups for years to come to help them continue to make sense in authentic ways throughout their tenures. It is a worthy investment in developing sensemaking processes, structures, and routines.

Ask Good Questions

Before you can make sense of the data with your team in a compelling way, it is vital to consider the inquiry questions that should guide the next level of review. These questions will help you discern which specific data sets, both quantitative and qualitative, and which types of analyses will be most helpful. In a school district, for example, these questions might include:

- How do we currently define excellence? What indicators matter most to our community?
- Based on this benchmark of excellence, what are our greatest strengths and challenges? What is our community most proud of or concerned about? Why?

- Where are we seeing the most improvement over time?
  Which schools are growing at a faster rate on the critical indicators of student performance that we care most about?
  What can we learn from them? What conditions have made
  this possible?
- Where are we seeing the most decline over time? Which
  schools are struggling the most on the indicators we care
  most about? What are the root causes? What conditions do
  they lack?
- Where are Asian, Black, Indigenous, and Latinx students seeing the most success on the indicators we care most about?
  What are the conditions that have made their success possible?
- Where are Asian, Black, Indigenous, and Latinx students experiencing the most difficulty with the indicators we care
  most about? What conditions are missing or serve as barriers
  to their success?
- What are the ripest opportunities for equity-focused change?

In a smaller team, you might articulate more narrow questions.
Consider the example of student attendance. The team might ask:
What does excellence in attendance mean for our community? Is it
simply showing up at school or class? Or is it more than that? Which
groups of students are struggling with attendance? Are there students within those same groups who are meeting the standard? Why?
What conditions exist that make their regular attendance possible?
What are the implications for our work?

From there, you can decide on which data sets and which analyses will help answer your questions and fuel your sensemaking discussion. Because data, especially quantitative data, has too often
been used to harm and oppress, it can surface strong emotions and
be triggering for marginalized communities. That said, there is important information in quantitative data that shouldn't be dismissed.
Quantitative data can reveal trends, but it doesn't tell you why those

trends exist, so it cannot be reviewed in isolation. That is why a balance of quantitative and qualitative data, as interpreted by the people represented in the numbers, is crucial. New leaders must be prepared to decide what data sources to use and also what methodologies are to be used for analysis.[8] The following tips can be used as a starting point for how to work with the data that has been collected:

- *Establish a benchmark for excellence.* At some point, the organization will set goals, but we think it is essential to anchor this discussion in a broad understanding of what your community values most. Without some initial calibration around what excellence means, it is hard to judge the data you will review.
- *Disaggregate the data.* It is important to disaggregate data by race, gender, and other demographic variables to develop a comprehensive picture of how various groups are situated relative to access and opportunity. But stopping there, as we often do, is dangerous. Equity-focused leaders should make more thoughtful comparisons that reveal actionable insights beyond the comparison of demographic groups.
- *Make comparisons.* Comparisons, which combine two or three observations, can produce new understandings.[9] Comparisons between similar schools with similar demographics or conditions can help us see progress where it might have otherwise been masked. Making comparisons within a demographic group can be particularly revealing when using quantitative and qualitative data together, as it can bring to the surface conditions that either obstruct or support student success.
- *Look at data over time.* It is essential to look at growth, as opposed to simple snapshots in time, but be careful about how it is done, especially with state assessment results that focus on the percentage of students considered "proficient." As assessment expert Andrew Ho warns, looking at these

percentages is like "viewing progress through a funhouse mirror." That is because, as Ho explains, proficiency is an arbitrary marker, and perceptions of growth (or decline) can be distorted depending on how close a district or school's performance is to the marker, which can also lead to misinterpretations related to gaps in achievement.[10] Consider exploring more appropriate methodologies, such as using scaled scores. Nevertheless, looking for trends is essential.

- *Look for outliers.* By using data visualizations, like scatter plots or quadrant plots, you can begin to see more easily the exceptions from which you can learn. Where are the surprises? Which schools, teachers, or grade levels serve Black and Brown students better than the rest? What new questions can you pursue?
- *Code your data.* When coding your qualitative data to look for themes, be sure to involve multiple people, preferably with different perspectives, to guard against biases. We also suggest that participant data from nondominant groups be coded separately so as not to lose their voices in the more extensive data set.

Most importantly, please resist the urge, or the pressure, to misuse data. While perhaps easier to explain, oversimplifying data can make it seem like some schools or students are performing better than others, and some performing worse—even when they aren't. As equity-focused leaders, we need to understand these pitfalls and help our communities use the available data appropriately.

Shift the Discourse

Once you have the data, it is time to work with your team to understand it and ultimately tell a story. But how we talk matters, and schools have historically engaged in discourse that reinforces the status quo.[11] If we are not careful, the stories we tell about the data will only confirm adult biases and therefore reinforce or even expand negative stereotypes about marginalized communities and families. Developing a compassionate understanding through data analysis requires leaders to pay close attention to language and shift the discourse.

Discourse is how we talk together, write, and represent things, and how we make meaning that informs and influences our decisions and actions. In the article "Changing the Discourse in Schools," Eugene Eubanks and his colleagues explain that there are two distinctive kinds of discourse in schools that either maintain or disrupt negative biases and stereotypes.[12] Discourse I, which is the dominant discourse in schools, is a hegemonic cultural discourse that reinforces inequity patterns. For example, you might hear an emphasis on singular truths about the data and see a focus on symptoms, the needs of adults, and the many constraints that exist.[13] Discourse II challenges ingrained assumptions by naming inequitable conditions and pushing to interrogate them in service of getting to more transformational approaches. For example, in a conversation characterized by Discourse II, you might hear multiple stories about the data, root-cause analyses, an emphasis on students' experiences, and a desire to get started despite constraints.[14] As leaders, we need not only to recognize and change the discourse we hear, but we need to learn to recognize our own. As you listen and participate in the sensemaking process, ask every participant to pay attention:

- How are people talking about the issue (disparities, neighborhoods, students, families) at hand? What are you hearing? What questions are we asking?
- What do you believe to be true about the issue?
- What assumptions are being made about the issue at hand?
- What positive assumptions can be made instead to interrupt negative assumptions?
- What actions would these positive assumptions produce?

As you establish norms, protocols, and roles (such as facilitator, note-taker, etc.) for your sensemaking sessions, consider the design with attention to discourse. One key role we often establish in meetings, for example, is the "process observer." Usually, this person checks on the extent to which participants abide by their group norms. But what if the group agreed to assign several people to pay attention to discourse? The goal here is to practice a new way of talking, thinking, and planning that leads to compassionate understanding.

A SKILL: ATTENTION TO COMPLEXITY

As we write this, we realize that a recurring theme in this chapter is one about attention to complexity. One framework that we have found to be helpful in our work as leaders is the Cynefin framework, a sensemaking model for leaders to "understand their challenges and make decisions in context" (see table 6.1).[15] The sensemaking process requires that we resist oversimplification, linear thinking, and our desires for clear causality because so many equity-focused problems we face are complex. David Snowden, who developed the framework, explains that through sensemaking, a leader must cultivate situational awareness to discern the kind of challenge one faces because problems in different types of contexts require unique responses.[16]

In leadership entry, we believe this is essential. Some of the problems we face will be clear and solved easily using best practices because there is a known cause and effect. Others will be complicated, and while difficult because more than one correct answer is possible, they can be solved over time and likely with support from experts. Some will be chaotic, as in a crisis that requires leaders to act before doing anything else. But many of the equity-focused challenges we face are complex, where the answers are unclear and the work is emergent. As new leaders, we must be able to share with our communities—by telling the story of our data—the kinds of problems we face and what it will take to solve them.

TABLE 6.1 Summary of the Cynefin framework

CONTEXT CHARACTERISTICS	APPROACH TO LEADERSHIP
Clear: Characterized by clear cause-and-effect relationships that are easily discernable by everyone.	A leader should sense, **categorize**, and then respond; apply "best" practices; rigid constraints exist.
Complicated: There exist multiple right answers, and though there is a clear relationship between cause and effect, not everyone can see it.	A leader should sense, **analyze**, and then respond; apply "good" practices; governing constraints exist.
Complex: Right answers do not exist, and there is no clear relationship between cause and effect; unpredictable.	A leader should **probe**, sense, and then respond; experiments lead to emergent practice; enabling constraints are needed to support innovation.
Chaotic: Searching for the right answer is pointless. The relationship between cause and effect is impossible to determine amid turbulence.	A leader should **act**, sense, and then respond; actions produce novel practice; there are no constraints.

Source: David J. Snowden and Mary E. Boone, "A Leader's Framework for Decision Making," *Harvard Business Review*, November 2007, https://hbr.org/2007/11/a-leaders-framework-for-decision-making; "Getting Started with Cynefin," (video), Cynefin Company, https://thecynefin.co/about-us/about-cynefin-framework/

In our experience, if we overpromise (through wishful thinking, a misdiagnosis, or a failure to diagnose altogether) and let people believe that a problem is complicated or straightforward when it is actually complex, we will find ourselves in trouble. The community, for example, may begin to demand that we "fix it" when the problem cannot be easily fixed. Similarly, if we make things out to be more complex than they are, we can find ourselves stuck, mired unnecessarily in process. A leader's preferred leadership style can influence how they categorize problems, so this sensemaking must be done with others.[17] As you make sense with your community and identify the most significant problems to solve, we encourage you to use the tool presented in table 6.2, based on the Cynefin framework, to explore multiple hypotheses and test assumptions.[18]

TABLE 6.2 Problem categorization tool

What are the big problems that have surfaced in your sensemaking?	What kind of problem is it (clear, complicated, complex, or chaotic) based on context? How do you know?	What are the implications for how you tell the data story to your community?

FINAL REFLECTION

In our own experience, sensemaking is a crucial but often overlooked step in the leadership entry process. For each of us, we wish we had done more of it before being swept up in the impetus to start planning for change. But it is the place where organizational growth occurs and should not be glossed over in our urgency to move to action. Slowing down, making sense, and testing assumptions is the common courtesy, as Toldson puts it, that all our communities deserve, especially those organizational and community members who have been marginalized.

Building compassionate understanding requires leaders to reimagine what data they collect, how they display it, and how to make sense of it. It requires that they disrupt data-driven dialogue and analysis that perpetuates bias. It necessitates attention to complexity.

Ultimately, to make this shift, we must see the humanity in people, including ourselves, and lift the experiences and voices of our students and families. Most importantly, by seeking a compassionate understanding, we are more likely to see the unique gifts, talents, and strengths that exist, on which we can collectively build.

As you plan for your leadership entry, consider these reflective questions:

- What are your inquiry questions?
- Who will help you make meaning of the data?
- What data sets will you focus on, and what types of analyses will you employ? How might you display the data in ways that produce new insight?
- How do you build empathy into your dialogue about the data?

CHAPTER 7

CHANGING THE NARRATIVE

Vision means seeing what could be and living the difference.
—AVESON SCHOOL OF LEADERS

Some of the leaders we spoke with entered communities that had experienced decades of disinvestment, and the dominant narrative focused on a vicious cycle of failure. Other leaders we interviewed entered communities that were largely satisfied with the status quo despite clear evidence that marginalized community members were not thriving. The dominant narrative was that there was no need to change. Either way, hope for better outcomes had dwindled as a result. Once a new leader has spent time listening, learning, and sensemaking, it is important that they share back to their communities what they heard. But this requires more than simply communicating a summary of strengths, challenges, and opportunities. The new leaders we interviewed used this opportunity to tell a new story, one that connects people to a cause and motivates them to make the change their organizations and communities deserve.[1]

Marshall Ganz, a community organizer who worked with Cesar Chavez and the United Farm Workers and helped design Barack Obama's 2008 grassroots organizing model, argues that narrative is crucial to change efforts. A leader must connect values and strategy through emotion to generate collective action. In his framework, he emphasizes the importance of telling one's own story to demonstrate authentic motivation, the story of the community to demonstrate their collective power and purpose, and the story of what a community or organization must do to make positive change. He calls these the story of self, the story of us, and the story of now.[2]

- *The Story of Self.* A story of self is personal. It is a story that demonstrates why you are motivated to do what it is you have been called to do and elucidates the values that drive you.[3] In leadership entry, we believe it is critical for a leader to communicate their values early and often and explain why they chose to lead in this place, at this time, and in this way. When a leader can introduce those values through a compelling story, as opposed to a bulleted list, it can be even more powerful. By doing so, the leader can begin to build trust by demonstrating competence, vulnerability, and moral purpose early on.

- *The Story of Us.* The story of us is a story that articulates what community members or members of an organization have in common, with a focus on their shared values.[4] In leadership entry, we believe it is critical that the leader show that they have seen and heard the community for who they are, the values they share, the assets they bring, the work they've done, and the challenges they face. After listening to and learning from one's community members, a new leader is well positioned to identify the connections and commonalities that can unite them around a shared purpose.

- *The Story of Now.* The story of now communicates the specific, urgent challenges or choices the members of the community must face to realize their purpose.[5] In leadership entry, we believe that sharing back with honesty a community or organization's biggest challenges provides an essential bridge from the listening and learning phase of entry to the action planning phase. By sharing these big challenges, obstacles that a community can overcome if they work together, the leader offers a clear invitation to share responsibility for change.

The focus of this chapter is on how leaders change the narrative about individuals, groups, organizations, and communities and mobilize them toward new possibilities. In it, we center the story of Kam Gordon, a first-year principal with the New York City Department of Education.[6] Through Kam's story we will examine the actions leaders can take early in the role to tell an honest and true narrative about the community they serve. We will then share implications for leadership entry and a skill to support new leaders in crafting narratives that honor a community and inspire positive change.

LEADERSHIP AS A LOVE LETTER TO THE COMMUNITY

WBHS, nestled in a park along a commercial street in the Bronx, launched in the summer of 2020. Kam Gordon began her leadership of the school in March, a few months before the school opened, to plan and prepare for the upcoming year. But on her first day, the New York City Department of Education (NYCDOE) stopped in-person instruction in response to the COVID-19 pandemic. Kam immediately found herself responsible for building a community and rallying a team that never had the chance to be in the same physical space together.

In the Bronx, many believe that one must leave the community to access opportunity and to receive an excellent education. In 2018, NYCDOE Chancellor Richard Carranza and Executive Superintendent Meisha Porter announced the "Bronx Plan" as an initiative aimed to redefine what was possible for youth within the borough.[7] This desire to change how the Bronx was viewed by both the community and the larger world was critical to the mission of WBHS and to Kam. As she prepared to meet the first cohort of students, a group she called "the founders," she anticipated cocreating with them new stories about the opportunity to learn in the Bronx.

For Kam, serving WBHS students well was personal. The daughter of Jamaican–West Indian immigrants and a Bronx native,

Kam grew up leaving for school at 6 a.m. so that she could take three buses to a private all-girls Catholic school outside her community. While this school provided excellent educational experiences, it was a place where few girls looked like Kam, who identifies as Black and of Caribbean descent. As she reflects on this time in her life, Kam notes, "I was trading my community and culture to access opportunity." She hoped that WBHS could be a place where kids could get a great education within walking distance of their homes. Leaning on the richness and cultural capital in the Bronx, Kam wanted the school to be one where youth would celebrate their culture, help their community flourish, and engage in deep and connected learning. A special education teacher and assistant principal who has spent her entire career working in the Bronx, Kam entered her role as principal with the goal of making WBHS a "love letter" to her community.

The beginning of the year virtual open-house meetings were one of the first opportunities Kam had to meet families. She used the time to talk about her experiences as both a learner and an educator. She invited family members into the mission of the school. Kam shared with families her belief that no one is a monolith, that all of us have multiple identities, and that school should be a place where everyone feels safe enough to show up in their entirety. For the more skeptical parents, Kam told stories of the work she had already done and the results she had achieved in the neighborhood as an educator. For many families, Kam's success story and the promise of WBHS was a breath of fresh air.

In these early gatherings, Kam prioritized her story. However, she also knew she had to hear the stories of those choosing WBHS and learn about what they needed. This would help her weave together a communal story. To help, she began a regular virtual "coffee with the principal" so that families could share their perspectives. Some moms shared how overwhelmed they felt—so much was happening in their lives and much of the work fell on them. While these conversations surfaced individual challenges, they also elevated the promise of their ability to support one another as a community. So Kam and the school decided to create space for parents to connect with and take care of one another through paint nights, wellness nights, and fitness activities, tapping into other facets of their identity beyond their individual roles as caregivers.

Beginning with her initial letter to students, an excerpt of which is included below (see the box "Kam Gordon's Welcome Letter to Students"), Kam also focused on telling a new story about what it meant to be a student at WBHS. She wanted to communicate that they had the agency to create the culture of the school. She wanted to stress the significance of student voice and feedback. Mostly, she wanted students to know they could be "problem solvers and change agents." These efforts did not stop at words but were embedded throughout the first-year curriculum. During the first year, for example, students interviewed their families and shared those stories in the classroom. They wrote and performed *I Am* poems in order to share aspects of their identity with peers and educators.[8] Through their own storytelling, they demonstrated the many assets they were bringing to this new school community.

These kinds of activities, focused on recognizing assets and uplifting values, were offered to teachers as well. Teachers communicated big ideas about the defining moments in their lives and professional growth through visual journey line presentations.[9] They also interviewed each other about what anti-racism, a core tenet of the school, looked like for them. Teachers then listened to and reflected on these interviews at the end of the year to see how they had grown as a school community committed to advancing equity.

It was important, too, for the school community to know more about the larger community in which they were embedded, so Kam and educators from WBHS identified other organizations they could learn from in order to enrich their understanding of the Bronx. For example, they met with South Bronx Rising Together, a

KAM GORDON'S
WELCOME LETTER TO STUDENTS

Dear WBHS Founders:

"We are the ones that we've been waiting for." —June Jordan

We are deeply honored that you chose to begin the journey into your adolescence as a founding member of WBHS. While we may be experiencing challenging times in our community, the country, and the world, we are a community that will overcome it together. Recent events have reminded us of why our mission at WBHS is all the more important. As our Founders, you will be a part of bringing this mission to life. You are all smart, strong, resilient, and capable, but even more exciting is the untapped potential that each of you will bring to our community. You will be celebrated for your individuality and creativity, and recognized for everything that makes you . . . YOU. Your voice is important, you matter, you belong. As we officially prepare to open the doors to welcome you into our new community, we would like to hear from you. We will soon reach out to learn more about how you envision your high school experience.

Our promise to you is that we will provide you with an experience unlike anything you have experienced before. In collaboration with your teachers and community allies, we will bring you an approach that pushes your thinking about what school is and could be and immerse you in activities that give you a new sense of purpose. We believe the best preparation for the real world is the real world and our five challenge areas, Applied Academics, Internships, Service Learning, Wilderness and Presentation, will engage your mind, spark your curiosity and extend your ambition beyond what you have ever imagined. We are problem solvers and change agents that will disrupt injustices, and we are connectors that will bring people together for common causes of justice. I am so excited to watch as you spread your wings and show the world the promise of The Bronx.

This is our Moment. This is the X. This is WBHS.

With Hope & Love,
Kam Gordon, Principal

community-based organization building pathways for youth from "cradle to college." The discussion, which also focused on problems they were seeing, produced some early wins and set the foundation for future work and collaboration.

What ultimately began to emerge was a much richer collective vision for WBHS that led to some initial priority areas and actions. The stories Kam heard helped her see that while there was a commitment to culturally responsive teaching, they needed to learn how to bring it to life. Together, they began to dive into Gholdy Muhammad's book *Cultivating Genius: An Equity Framework for Culturally and Historically Responsive Literacy* to learn about how to put their vision of instruction into action.[10] Kam also gleaned from these stories that there was a shared commitment to collaboration, as they all knew that enacting their vision would require working together hand in hand. As such, they prioritized common planning to make sure that no teacher was working in isolation. Finally, she could see that their vision would only come to life if they continued to cultivate and elevate the brilliance of their students. So they looked for every opportunity to tell the stories of WBHS and their students in the larger community.

Looking back on the first year of her leadership and her entry activities, Kam remains an optimistic champion for the school and for the Bronx. She takes pride in the ways in which the school has built its culture around the stories of its students and how it is collectively changing the narrative about what is possible in the South Bronx. She also acknowledges that they are still in the rising action of the narrative and that there is much work to be done. Kam continues to ask herself and others, "What is the true story of this organization and the community it serves?" It is a narrative in progress, and one that imagines new possibilities for the people who live and learn there.

OUR ANALYSIS

Elements of Marshall Ganz's three stories to motivate collective action are peppered throughout Kam's approach to entry. The following section highlights how Kam used the stories of self, us, and now to create a vision at WBHS.

Stories of Self

As Kam Gordon entered her role, she reflected on her values, her identity, and her history so that she could communicate to others why she should lead, why this school, and why this moment. She shared her own story as proof of what is possible when one harnesses the resilience, talent, and wisdom of one's community, and she connected that story through common language to the mission of WBHS. What was most effective about Kam's use of storytelling, however, was that even when telling her story, she did not center herself in the work. She used her story to make connections to the community she serves, building trust through her demonstration of competence, vulnerability, and commitment to their success.

Stories of Us

Kam also elevated the stories of her new school community members and drew connections between them, which was especially critical in a school community that was forming during a crisis. By engaging staff, students, and families in storytelling activities, Kam was able to identify and highlight common interests and evidence of shared purpose. Even more important, members of her school community were able to witness and celebrate their many strengths. Whether it was parents celebrating their cultural wealth, students sharing their hopes and dreams, or teachers sharing their vision for excellent instruction, Kam began to help people see their collective strength and a possible future as a school.

Stories of Now

Kam used the story of self and the story of us to create legitimacy and communal energy. She then directed that energy toward action through the story of now. Her priorities, which focused on culturally responsive teaching, collaboration, and student voice, required everyone to contribute their efforts. She communicated specific actions her community could take to achieve their collective vision. Teachers understood why they would have to work differently and took risks to make their practice public. Students embraced the opportunity to share what mattered to them and to lead their learning. Even the community was inspired to act on behalf of the school vision. For example, when the state of New York proposed holding the traditional Regents examinations during the pandemic, families and community members advocated for a different approach at WBHS, one better aligned to the values and priorities of the school. By changing the narrative about her school, she inspired collective action.

IMPLICATIONS FOR LEADERS

In leadership entry, it is critical to share back what you think you have learned about the organization with a focus on strengths, challenges, and opportunities. You owe it to your community to do so. This can be done through formal presentations and reports, and it can also take place in elevators and faculty lounges. The key is to use this opportunity to change the narrative. Leaders must share difficult truths coupled with hopeful pictures of the future, shape their communication choices based on audience, and reframe negative narratives through strengths-based language.

Speak Truth and Speak to the Future

During leadership entry, it is critical to name the organization's strengths on which to build. But equity-focused leaders must also speak about hard truths, explain why the organization must change, and admit to how difficult it will be to do so. Telling these truths can be challenging when so many of the problems we face are rooted in racism. Engaging oneself and others in ongoing discussions about the manifestations of racism in your organization requires an ability to make space for shame, grief, anger, and other emotions while remaining resolute in the need for change. It necessitates a constant evaluation and adjustment of how much unsettling of the status quo the community can bear. Most leaders will wrestle with self-doubt that they aren't doing enough or pushing hard enough because the problems are urgent. But it starts with naming them. As James Baldwin said, "Not everything that is faced can be changed, but nothing can be changed until it is faced."

Change is so hard because it requires loss, and new leaders must talk openly about that. According to leadership experts Ronald Heifetz and Marty Linsky, "You need to respect and acknowledge the loss that people suffer when you ask them to leave behind something they have lived with for years. It is not enough to point to a hopeful future. People need to know that you realize that the change you are asking them to make is difficult and what you are asking them to give up has real value to them."[11] What we value and protect so often is our perceptions of ourselves. We want to believe we are good people who have done everything we can. We want to retain our reputations as intelligent and effective. We want to protect ourselves from being perceived as racist or complicit in racism. We fear failure. Being asked to change can directly threaten our individual and collective identities, even when we know it is for the better. For that reason, it is critical to acknowledge the loss that comes with change.

But it is not enough to speak to the present challenges and the change that must come. A new leader must paint a picture of a better future, too. While there are degrees of loss in this evolution, there is much more to gain if we hold onto a shared vision. To be clear, speaking to future possibilities is not about painting pictures while wearing rose-colored glasses, but about pointing toward the genuine aspirations of one's community. As you craft the narrative for your entry report, give people solid ground on which to stand by speaking the truth about the present, acknowledge how hard it will be to change, but offer your community a better future as defined by them. This touchstone will give them a reason to work through the turbulence of change.

Interrupt Negative Narratives and Use Strengths-Based Language

As you speak to members of the community and, more importantly, as you listen to them, you will hear stories and perspectives that represent a deficit view. Some people will talk poorly about colleagues, about students, about teachers, and about the organization or community. Sometimes these are deeply held beliefs and other times these comments reflect the speaker's sense of powerlessness to effect change. Effective equity-focused leaders use entry to push on negative narratives in healthy ways by anticipating and interrupting them with strengths-based language.

One of the most common ways leaders combat negative narratives is to immerse themselves and others in the counter narratives. As you meet people, where are you seeing proof points of what is possible? Collect and treasure those stories. Memorize those names and share those tales far and wide. Talk about the excellent teachers and lessons you've observed working in schools with poor reputations. Interview kids who graduated from college who were not expected to make it through high school. Figure out who your community's secret champions and business sector advocates are and share how they support the broader vision. There are always stories available in every community that offer evidence that change is possible.

As you gather these stories, ensure that you do so in a way that honors and respects their dignity. Only share stories with permission and in a way that doesn't embarrass the protagonist or shame the listener. Ask and consider whether stories should be told with or without attribution, and consider whether telling the story will open someone up to attack. White and male leaders should take special caution to ensure they do not appropriate ideas and strategies of women and people of color without ensuring they receive the credit and reward. Finally, ensure your stories do not reduce people and their actions to stereotypes or cartoon versions of themselves.

The best stories honor our complexity and elevate the value and good in people.

While it is through one-on-one and small group interactions that you will have opportunities to identify and interrupt negative narratives, over time you will notice patterns. You can use strengths-based language to strategically introduce new ways of talking about the work, the organization, and the people within the community. Before you consider how best to communicate what you've learned through your entry process, reflect on the language you've heard in the field that perpetuates negative narratives, deficit thinking, or stereotypes, perhaps especially about students of color and their families. For some examples, see table 7.1. How might you disrupt deficit thinking, language, and perceptions in your communication every step of the way as a leader?

TABLE 7.1 Examples of deficit and corresponding strengths-based language

DEFICIT LANGUAGE	STRENGTHS-BASED LANGUAGE
These families never attend district forums or community events.	Our parents are busy people with competing priorities, including how they use their limited free time. We must change our own practices to meet their discerning bar.
With all our students must deal with outside of school, it is enough for school to be a place where they are loved.	Our students receive all kinds of love at home, in the community, and at school. The highest form of school love is the belief that each student is capable of excellence and deserving of deep learning and critical feedback.
You must leave this community if you are going to be successful and safe.	There are assets in our community that remain untapped. The health of our community depends on our students becoming our future teachers, leaders, and engaged residents.
Our goal is to close the achievement gap.	Our goal is for each and every student to realize their potential. That will require that we change the systems that reproduce racialized outcomes.

Be Intentional in How You Deliver Messages of Change

In addition to crafting content that speaks to the truth and the future using strengths-based language, leaders must also think carefully about how to communicate their entry findings to a variety of community members. This requires aligning their message, medium, and audience. We suggest that you start by creating a report or presentation that summarizes your leadership entry findings. From there, adapt the information or presentation based on the specific message you want to send and the intended audience using the communication tools at your disposal. Some leaders make good use of email, newsletters, social media applications, and texts to get the word out. These tools can reach a large audience, be translated into multiple languages, and provide clear and useful information. Other leaders might lean into videos, podcasts, phone calls, or public events. These formats allow for people to see you and your personality, provide opportunities for more interaction, and bring in other voices. Just be cognizant of the need for interpretation, possibly in multiple languages. Ideally, you will incorporate some combination of these one-way and two-way communication mechanisms. Most importantly, this report or presentation, adapted in ways that make sense, creates direction for the organization and holds the leader accountable.

A SKILL: WRITING YOUR ENTRY REPORT

Ensuring that your entry process benefits as many people as possible and that the learning and future efforts are owned by a broad coalition is critical to success. A documented report and presentation about your entry also allows you to hold yourself accountable to the commitments you make by communicating them publicly with updates on your achievements. Below is an outline you can adapt and use to engage students, faculty, or community members in sharing learning from your entry process in order to tell new stories and mobilize for collective action (see the box "Outline of an Entry Report").

OUTLINE OF AN ENTRY REPORT

A formal entry report is typically five to fifteen pages, depending on the role, and it describes the entry process, summarizes the key insights and learning from entry, names potential priorities moving forward, and outlines the process for developing a strategy and action plan, if appropriate.

LETTER OF INTRODUCTION AND OBJECTIVES OF YOUR ENTRY PLAN:
- Reiterate your background, values, and reason for accepting the role.
- Articulate what equity means to you and the implications for your leadership.
- Reiterate the goals for your entry process. Articulate both what you hoped to learn and what you planned to accomplish through the process.

METHODOLOGY:
- Review the process used to engage with the organization during your entry period.
- Summarize the key actions you took and the information sources you explored as part of your learning.
- Provide the questions you asked during interviews that shaped your thinking.
- Share who helped you make sense of the data you gathered.

STRENGTHS, CHALLENGES, OPPORTUNITIES, AND EMERGING PRIORITIES:
- Celebrate the strengths and assets of the organization that are most relevant to future success.
- Highlight the major challenges and opportunities.
- List three to five major emerging priorities for the organization and your rationale for prioritizing them.

NEXT STEPS:
- If appropriate, share who you will be working with to develop a strategy to address the emerging priorities.
- Share when your community can expect to hear more.

CONTACT INFORMATION:
- Share a way in which people can provide feedback on your entry report.
- Close with a note of gratitude and appreciation.

DESIGN POSSIBILITIES:
- Photos, links to videos, data displays, and icons can help to personalize your plan and ensure readers take away the most important information.
- Consider including quotes that inspire you, connect to your plan, or capture a key insight you heard from people during your entry process.
- Be clear about what you know and what you are still uncovering. Include essential questions and wonderings that will guide your work in the future.
- Name specific people and organizations who helped with the development of your entry report.

FINAL REFLECTION

The past decade in politics has reminded us that how we communicate matters. We can use our words to inspire hope and release unrealized potential as much as we can use them to stoke fear and hate. In each of our experiences with leadership entry, we took advantage of the disruption caused by leadership change to say things that might have ordinarily gone unsaid. We tried to lift the voices of our communities and speak to their values. We named their many strengths and the progress that had already been made. We also named the biggest challenges and opportunities. If we could do it again, however, we would have told more stories from the beginning, including our own. We would have been more intentional about changing the deficit narrative that exists in too many school districts, schools, and related organizations. And we would have told a more compelling story about our collective vision for the future from the start. Sharing what you've learned during leadership entry presents an extraordinary opportunity to tell a new narrative, one that connects a community and motivates positive change.

As you plan for your leadership entry, consider these reflective questions:

- How might you communicate the values of your community? What are their collective hopes and dreams?
- What are the greatest gifts and assets your organization or community has to offer? If you could only say good things, what would you say?
- What are the greatest challenges that stand in the way? How would you describe their history and their current manifestations?
- How might you disrupt deficit thinking, language, and perceptions in your communication every step of the way as a leader?
- What are your top-line messages? How will you communicate your findings in a way that invites reflection and motivates collective action?

CHAPTER 8

GALVANIZING FOR ACTION

Action on behalf of life transforms. Because the relationship between self and the world is reciprocal, it is not a question of first getting enlightened or saved and then acting. As we work to heal the earth, the earth heals us.

—ROBIN WALL KIMMERER

In our empathy interviews with equity-focused leaders, several moved seamlessly from their entry activities into strategy development and action planning. Once a new leader has gathered deep insight into the organization's strengths, challenges, and possibilities and built stronger, trusting relationships, it makes good common sense to use this trust and understanding to plan for the future. In some cases, a leader will develop a new strategy, and in others, they may adopt an existing one.

But strategic planning is notoriously flawed. As Liz City and Rachel Curtis describe in their book, *Strategy in Action*, strategic plans are too often focused on compliance and not innovation, designed to communicate to an external audience rather than to engage an internal one, and filled with lists of initiatives instead of a few interdependent strategies aimed at sustainable change.[1] In our experience, an insular team often carries out strategic planning without deep consideration of past efforts or sufficient planning for the ways of working needed to implement the strategy in a complex environment.

For these reasons and more, we want to distinguish our emphasis on "strategy development" from traditional strategic planning.

Stacey Childress, who also studies strategy development in public schools, says a well-crafted strategy:

- *Connects to purpose.* People responsible for executing the actions chosen by the organization can readily see a link to the mission and objectives in their work.
- *Provides focus.* People at all levels understand who their customers are, what service they are providing to them, and why.
- *Guides choices.* People throughout the organization can make better choices between possible activities, projects, and programs by assessing their fit with the strategy.
- *Illuminates relationships.* People understand how their actions are related to the actions of others in the organization and are able to recognize and take advantage of linkages and interdependencies to accomplish objectives.
- *Defines measurement parameters.* People can work together to identify measures that are focused on the organizational learning necessary for continuous improvement of activities related to the strategy, and can create and track indicators of performance relevant to successful execution of the strategy.
- *Addresses the external environment.* People are focused on the work of the organization, but understand how it links to the external context and the expectations of stakeholders.
- *Allows for adaptation.* Leaders in the organization are able to adapt the strategy as the organization learns about the effectiveness of activities through implementation and monitoring and/or in response to changes in the external environment.[2]

However, we would emphasize that *equity-focused* strategy development also requires a set of critical mindsets that set it apart, dispositions that are necessary to galvanize a community to put a strategy into action. Researchers Ann Ishimaru and Mollie Galloway developed a conceptual framework for organizational leadership for educational equity that highlights three critical drivers that distinguish exemplary equitable leadership practice.[3]

- *Framing of disparities and actions.* This driver describes how a leader understands educational disparities. Rather than frame the problem through a deficit lens or oversimplify it as a lack of opportunity, the authors assert that exemplary leaders for equity "see the institution and institutional racism as responsible for disparities, own their role in perpetuating institutional practices, and seek transformation of the system."[4]

  As a new leader transitions from sensemaking into strategy development, it is crucial that they name the systemic problems that emerged through their entry process and how they are rooted in history. Only then can they collaboratively explore those problems and their root causes with the people who are most experiencing them. Spending time on problem identification and root-cause analysis will ensure that related strategies have the potential for positive impact.

- *Construction and enactment of leadership.* This driver describes how participation and decision-making are enacted. Rather than drive decision-making from a position of authority, an exemplary equity-focused leader "builds the capacity of staff, students, parents, and community members to engage in meaningful collaboration and authentically shares power and decision making."[5]

  New leaders must work collaboratively with a team on strategy development, ideally drawing on some of the people who participated in their entry process, including those the organization serves. Too often, young people, along with their parents and teachers, are left out of the strategy development process entirely. We leaders assume that the work is too technical and filled with education jargon for them to engage meaningfully. However, an equity-focused leader works hard to include their voices even during strategy development, as coconstruction will result in better ideas and a shared commitment to bringing those ideas to life.

- *Inquiry culture.* This driver describes ongoing inquiry and continuous improvement processes informed by quantitative and qualitative data. Rather than make ongoing decisions and adjustments to a strategy based on assumptions or personal values, an exemplary leader for equity engages in an "ongoing cycle of inquiry with members of the entire school community using multiple forms of data."[6]

New leaders who move into strategy development and action planning must also plan for ongoing rigorous improvement cycles. They must continually amplify what is working, tamp down what isn't, and problem-solve when necessary. Most importantly, these routines should include regular opportunities to gain insight from people with different perspectives in order to drive change.

This chapter highlights Jennifer (Jen) Cheatham's collaborative development of both her original strategy in 2013 and then a new strategy in 2018 as the superintendent of the Madison Metropolitan School District in Madison, Wisconsin.[7] After four years of implementation and adaptation of a strategy born out of her initial leadership entry process, she and her team decided to reenact a yearlong leadership entry process to refresh the district's strategy and to galvanize her community for the next level of change. We think this example will be instructive for new leaders who are developing an initial strategy as well as for experienced leaders who may be pivoting their strategy or taking it to the next level. We will then analyze her work, emphasizing Ishimaru and Galloway's drivers for equitable leadership, identify implications, and offer a critical skill related to effective strategy development. Ultimately, we hope this story will help you consider how to motivate your own community for meaningful change.

REENTRY FOCUSED ON NEXT LEVEL CHANGE

Jen's original mandate from the Madison community in 2013 was simple to explain, but she knew it would be challenging to execute given that she was entering at a time of low trust and that there were fears that she was an outside reformer from Chicago who would simply import her own strategy without building on community assets. Her job as she saw it in the beginning was to build community confidence, to provide direction, and to improve student performance, focusing on shrinking a decades-long "achievement gap" between Black and White students. The school district's strikingly large gap was of primary concern to those she spoke to, as racial disparities in the county between Black and White residents were described as some of the largest in the nation.[8] As local education scholar Gloria Ladson-Billings pointed out to Jen early on, Black youth were the "canaries in the coal mine" in Madison.[9] Their experiences reflected the health of the school system. If they were not thriving, then no one really was.

Developed with urgency by a collaborative planning team of school and district educators and informed by an intense community engagement period, the district's original strategy focused on school improvement planning, professional learning about excellent teaching, and a set of five priority areas for the central office. Simultaneously, she built a powerful and diverse team of senior leaders to help bring the strategy to life. While on the surface these levers might not have sounded like the makings of an equity strategy, the theory that informed them, made stronger and more explicit over time, was grounded in equitable practice and served as a prerequisite for the kind of transformational change they envisioned in the future.

The idea was that the district would not be able to make progress for all students, Black students in particular, if it were not more disciplined about its decision-making, more attuned to excellent teaching and learning that is culturally responsive, and more aggressive about providing the resources needed for schools to do their best work while tearing down institutional barriers that stood in their way. The strategy also committed the district to cycles of continuous improvement to promote organizational learning at every level; regular school visits to stay grounded in the classroom; and formal advisories to gain insight and guidance from students, teachers, parents, principals, and community leaders on systemwide efforts.[10] These strategies, they believed, would begin to address the gaps in opportunity that resulted in disparities in achievement.

While Jen hadn't put a time frame on the initial strategy, at the end of the 2016–17 school year, after four years of implementation, she and her leadership team could see that it would soon be time for a reboot. They had primarily achieved what they set out to do in this first phase of change, as evidenced by the district's clear direction, increased coherence, and steady progress on most student outcomes and in most schools.[11] But they could also see that some metrics, such as the extreme disparities between Black and White students in school discipline data, would not budge despite considerable effort, and they were frustrated. Many said the problem was in the implementation. But for Jen, it was more complex. In her experience, persistent problems like this one pointed to a lack of common understanding of the fundamental issues they were trying to address. These problems were rooted in systemic racism and in the absence of a shared commitment to act on them. She had come to believe that they would never make the change their students deserved without a more powerful shared vision, a deeper understanding of the real problems that stood in the way, and more equitable ways of working.

She also knew that more meaningful change for the young people she served would never happen if the district strategy was seen as hers alone. Recalling the invigorating experience of leadership entry and how it galvanized so many for change, Jen wondered what it would look like to reenact it. After consulting her team, her board, her principals, and her trusted advisory groups, she decided to launch what she called internally her "reentry" process (laid out in figure 8.1), an engagement process designed to motivate her community for the next level of work.[12]

FIGURE 8.1 Phases of Jen Cheatham's reentry plan

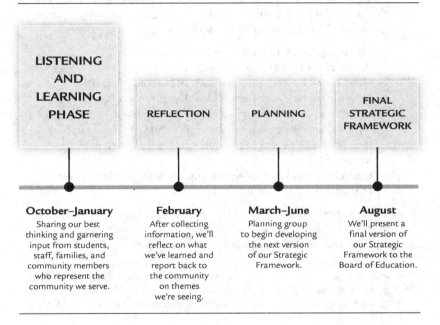

October–January
Sharing our best thinking and garnering input from students, staff, families, and community members who represent the community we serve.

February
After collecting information, we'll reflect on what we've learned and report back to the community on themes we're seeing.

March–June
Planning group to begin developing the next version of our Strategic Framework.

August
We'll present a final version of our Strategic Framework to the Board of Education.

In the first three months of the process, Jen focused on listening and learning, but this time with fresh ears and eyes, centering the voices of people of color and other historically marginalized groups in ways she hadn't originally.[13] Whether it was a school visit, focus group, or open forum, she shared some background, solicited ideas, and then shared her best thinking for feedback (see the box "Protocol for Listening Sessions"). She also hired a well-known and trusted community member to design a parallel process, in collaboration with her head of family, youth, and community engagement, to engage Black, Hmong, and Latinx parents and caregivers to expand the circle of influence and garner deeper insight. Monthly, Jen provided

PROTOCOL FOR LISTENING SESSIONS

In each of her sessions, Jen provided some grounding in where the district had been in the last five years, and then participants brainstormed in small groups using the following prompt:

Imagine a time in the future when we are celebrating our progress—with dramatically more students on track to graduate college, career, and community ready. Imagine the actions we took to get there.

- Where did we build on our previous success?
- Where did we make bold moves?
- How did we best support you as staff? (asked of staff), or
- How did we best collaborate with the community? (asked of community members), or
- How did we best partner with parents and families to support their children? (asked of parents, caregivers, and family members), or
- How did we create strong relationships with students? (asked of students)

She then presented her thinking on a set of "big ideas" to guide the next strategic framework and asked for feedback on what seemed most promising and what they were most curious about.

Source: Beth Vaade and Amanda Jeppson, *Strategic Framework Engagement—Final Research Report on the Listening and Learning Phase* (Madison, WI: Research and Program Evaluation Office, Madison Metropolitan School District, 2018).

public updates on what was emerging from these conversations to ensure transparency.

While she heard plenty of things she had heard before, she remembers being struck by several of these powerful conversations. They crystallized for her why the district was stuck and what it would take to propel the work forward. They also pointed to a vision that she thought everyone would embrace.

When she talked to her teachers of color advisory group, for example, she recalls how they challenged the district to commit once and for all to becoming an anti-racist organization from the boardroom to the classroom. All policies, budget investments, and longtime ways of working had to be tested, deconstructed, and rebuilt. She remembers vividly a group of Black youth who said they didn't simply need more teachers of color. They needed stronger, more trusting relationships with teachers and staff, including with their White teachers. For them, trusting relationships with their teachers, counselors, and principals were a prerequisite for authentic learning in the classroom. She also distinctly remembers a group of Spanish-speaking Latinx parents who told her they wanted deeper and richer learning opportunities for their students, not just more programs or interventions to support struggling students. They didn't believe the curriculum was preparing their children for full participation in a multicultural world. Each discussion magnified manifestations—some technical and some adaptive—of a larger problem rooted in racism and oppression.

While these meetings resonated and clarified for Jen what it would take for every child to excel, she knew only shared understanding would lead to collective action. In the next phase, Jen engaged her advisory groups, her senior team, and the school board in making sense with her to build consensus on what they were hearing and then provide a formal summative report to the community. To fuel their discussion, she asked her qualitative research team to draw out and codify general themes from the data as well as critical nuances or differences surfaced by nondominant groups, focusing on people of color and students.

What emerged from the data were clear areas of continued focus, but with essential stipulations that further clarified the real problems that stood in the way.[14] For example, participants generally agreed that the district should stay focused on teaching and learning, especially in literacy. But Asian, Black, Indigenous, and Latinx students demanded a historically accurate and culturally representative curriculum as essential to the district's future efforts. While participants largely agreed that the district should remain focused on improving parent, youth, and community engagement, parents of color explained that engagement was not enough. In its next phase, the district needed to learn how to share power, especially between parents, students, and educators. These data, coupled with the insight garnered from over four years of implementation of the initial strategy, opened up honest conversations about the future they wanted to create, the problems they faced, and potential implications for strategy.

Informed by the codified themes from her listening and learning phase, Jen then moved into a collaborative strategy development process. Supported by her senior team, the group consisted of a racially diverse group of about eighty educators (teachers, principals, and central office staff), parents, and students from across the district, recruited mainly from her existing advisory groups, as they had engaged in every step of the process and would have the context to participate fully. Additionally, Jen hired an external facilitator who had experience with equity-focused strategy development. As shown in figure 8.2, they began with a whole group meeting on the district's theory of change and strategy levers. Once they agreed on these areas, participants signed up for a small group based on their interests to work on fleshing out each strategy lever into key initial actions. They then ended with another whole group meeting focused on coherence and alignment across strategic levers and ongoing ways of working.

FIGURE 8.2 Madison's process for strategy development

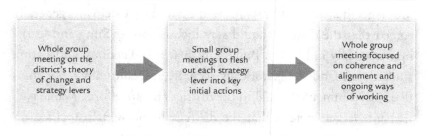

It was unusual for students, parents, and school-based staff to be so involved in the granular work of district strategy development, but the process made the strategy, and its rationale, stronger. The strategy levers they ultimately agreed on built on past efforts while addressing gaps in their initial theory. The new thinking was that for the district to move beyond incremental change, with a focus on Black youth, they would have to do more than embrace disciplined ways of working; they would have to fully empower school communities (including students and parents) to develop and drive school-based strategy. They would have to move beyond functioning as a community of practice focused on culturally responsive teaching and invest fully in people as anti-racist educators throughout the life of their employment. The central office would have to be more precise about their priority areas and propel work that promoted deep and rich learning, like the establishment of a historically accurate and representative curriculum.

The group also agreed that the district would have to adopt some new ways of working aimed at the next level of change. They'd have to begin working across institutions on long-term planning, something that was often dismissed because of turnover in leadership. They would have to build new skills around school- and community-based innovation so that they could design for the future in partnership with their community, grabbing onto emergent learning with an eye toward bringing it to scale, when appropriate. Most importantly, the group discussed what it would mean to become an anti-racist institution, one that would root out racist policies and practices while lifting and cultivating the brilliance of students of color, with a focus on Black youth. Jen recognized that she would also have to make significant changes in her leadership. The conversations that the community was having foreshadowed ways in which she had to think and act differently than she had been trained. She had to start to think beyond what was in her control and what could be accomplished during her tenure, and she would have to share power in ways that she had never seen demonstrated by another education leader.

In the end, after a full year of engagement, including ninety-six community meetings where over two thousand voices were heard, the school board and the senior team took one last look at the strategy they had outlined, knowing that they would be held accountable for following through on their promises.[15] They reviewed the district's vision, core values, and goals. They discussed the strategic shifts they were making in practice. And they surfaced initial implications for the district's commitment to Black Excellence (see the box "Black Excellence" below), born out of ongoing discussions with Black students, staff, and parents about what it would really take to transform the education system for every child.

BLACK EXCELLENCE

We believe in the brilliance, creativity, capability and bright futures of Black youth throughout Madison. Our measure of success as a school system must be aimed at more than narrowing gaps—but focused on cultivating the full potential of every child.

We believe that our strategy, informed by Black students, staff and families, has great potential to benefit Black youth. We also believe that we don't have all the solutions, which is why we must rally together as a community, working in deep and ongoing partnership with students, families and community members to disrupt the barriers that stand in our students' way. What does this mean? Creating space for healthy identity development, strategies to support academic excellence and new narratives about Black youth in Madison.

We'll start by creating a community coalition to support us in making this goal a reality. We believe that by designing new ways to care for and meet the social-emotional and academic needs of Black students, we will make our district and our community better for all.

Source: Madison Metropolitan School District Strategic Framework, https://go.boarddocs .com/wi/mmsd/Board.nsf/files/B3744G78E472/$file/Strategic%20Framework %20Final.pdf.

Most importantly, they came to understand that the strategy would continue to form as they learned. They asked themselves: How would they continue to seek insight? How would they do a better job of sharing decision-making power? How would they deal with resistance to their anti-racist stance? How would they help a predominantly White community see the expansive ways that Black students are brilliant and create a system that allows them to flourish? With knowledge that these questions weren't easily answered and would require ongoing dialogue, they sensed they were on the precipice of doing something together that would result in the real change their youth deserved.

OUR ANALYSIS

The process of deep listening, sensemaking, and communicating can transition a leader seamlessly into strategy development and action planning. But this story also demonstrates how the approaches we use during leadership entry can be extended throughout one's tenure and should never be reserved for just those first few months on the job. In this section, we explore more deeply how Jen utilized Ishimaru and Galloway's drivers for equitable leadership practice. And in each area of our analysis, we will incorporate additional details that demonstrate how she used her reentry process to galvanize her community for action.

Framing of Disparities and Actions

In the beginning, Jen reframed racial disparities as "opportunity gaps," though she became increasingly explicit over time about their root causes being historical and systemic—but she wondered if she could have gotten there faster. While most Asian, Black, Indigenous, and Latinx community members were deeply cognizant of this reality, Jen found that White community members generally struggled to recognize systemic racism and their part in it, and she worried that she spent too much time in the beginning catering to their needs and prioritizing their comfort. Over time, she learned that it was important to create intentional spaces for both envisioning the possibilities and understanding the problems that stood in the way, as both a sense of hopelessness and defensiveness could get in the way of real change. For her, slowing down to make sense was okay, but stopping was not. Leadership entry provided natural opportunities for within and cross-racial dialogue, and she took advantage of them.

For example, while Jen moved into strategy development in the second semester of the school year, she continued to conduct school visits and meet with other groups to test the themes that had emerged (a process called "member checks" in qualitative research). These conversations, especially those she had with predominantly White school staff, opened up dialogue not just about the potential shifts they might make, but about what it would take to become an anti-racist organization. While these discussions could be charged and emotional, they gave her increased confidence that district educators were largely ready to make this commitment systemwide. Most importantly, she could see how these spaces for dialogue, always reframing problems and learning together through action and reflection, would need to be part of the district's ongoing practice, as the impetus to return to old ways of thinking and doing the work would remain. Galvanizing her community for action would require slowing things down sometimes to make sense together so that they could propel their work forward.

Construction and Enactment of Leadership

While Jen certainly had ideas about what the district should work on next, which she openly shared, the district's strategy was coconstructed, building from the themes that emerged from the district's listening, learning, and sensemaking.[16] As a result, the strategy was more rooted in empowerment, supportive of risk-taking, and focused on trust and relationship building. Perhaps most vital, the strategy included attention to long-term cross-institutional planning (five, ten, and fifteen years out), which many people felt was woefully missing and essential to solving long-standing inequities in the areas of early childhood education, access to neighborhood resources, and school facilities. It would have been inauthentic for Jen and her leadership team, as experienced district leaders, not to have a point of view on the future strategy. But by bringing in a range of voices, especially students, school-based staff, parents, and community members, the strategy became much more powerful, tethered to problems worth solving and a vision worth achieving.

As a result of the engagement process, she had also become aware of the importance of partnering with the people who were doing the work of racial equity and social justice in the ongoing co-design of strategy. In fact, she shared that almost immediately after the approval of the new strategy, student activists surfaced gaps, pointing to the district's use of school resource officers as a strategy that flew in the face of Black Excellence, an issue that would become a major focus in the next year. She was interested in working more closely with student activists who were pushing the district beyond its comfort zone. She also wanted to do a better job of including community elders who could not only share insight about the history of change for racial justice, but who were still actively participating in it. And she wanted to include teachers, especially activist teachers and teachers of color, who were demanding more from the system, often taking the work into their own hands. While they had a different role to play, and were understandably resistant to working inside the system, she knew how important it was to work alongside them, authorizing their leadership whenever she could. Motivating change in her district would mean moving with the energy in her community.

Inquiry Culture

Jen had already established a culture of inquiry in the school district, but it didn't attend enough to complexity. Working with her board, her leadership team, her principals, and her advisory groups, they began a conversation about what it would mean to lead in an environment where the answers weren't always clear, in which there would be resistance to change, and in which learning was emergent. They agreed that ongoing reviews of progress would continue to be grounded in quantitative and qualitative data, but their sensemaking of the data would have to bring in the voices of the people behind the numbers to test their assumptions. Every cycle of inquiry would need to focus as much on their learning as their outcomes. And their decisions about scaling would have to happen with more intentionality and attention to grassroots efforts, not just those efforts led by administrators at the central office. Stimulating change would require grabbing onto learning in ways that hadn't been done in the past.

IMPLICATIONS FOR LEADERS

In addition to demonstrating the drivers for equitable leadership, we want to draw out a few actionable implications for new leaders who are considering moving into strategy development and action planning that may not have been demonstrated in the vignette.

Establish a More Robust Vision for Success

New leaders who transition into strategy development have an opportunity to establish a more robust vision for success that goes beyond typical promises to close the achievement gap. As Gloria Ladson-Billings stated in 2006, "I want to argue that this all-out focus on the 'Achievement Gap' moves us toward short-term solutions that are unlikely to address the long-term underlying problem."[17]

Our visions for success must be tethered to a larger commitment to the purpose of public schooling with a focus on self-actualization and participation in a democratic society. Related goals can be expanded beyond measures for reading and math to measures of wellness and belonging, since these are necessary ingredients for academic success. Bottom line, racial equity work is long and hard, and it won't last without a robust vision for success and a set of related goals worth pursuing, created with the community one serves.

Be Explicit About Problems and Their Manifestations

New leaders who segue into strategy development also have a window of opportunity to be more explicit about the problems that stand in the way of their visions for success, especially problems rooted in racism. In an opinion piece that Jen wrote with scholar John Diamond for *Education Week*, they said, "Too often, we educators soft-pedal this reality as if avoiding the racial elephant in the room would persuade certain powerful white people to listen to our messages. The best way forward is for educational leaders to challenge racial oppression boldly and directly."[18] Leadership change can provide the disruption necessary to say things that are hard to say.

But just as important is understanding the manifestations of the problem and their root causes so that we can create better solutions. While there are many good models for problem identification and root-cause analysis, we find ourselves returning to the Seven Circle model (developed by Steve Zuieback and Tim Dalmau based on the work of Margaret Wheatley, and adapted by the National Equity Project) as another helpful tool for problem exploration.[19] Identifying the problem's technical and relational manifestations, as well as exploring the environment in which the problem exists, can offer multipronged solutions that result in a more coherent strategy. We believe it is somewhere between a more robust vision for success and better understanding of the problem that strategy will emerge.

Establish New Ways of Reporting on Progress

New leaders who transition into strategy development and action planning can also establish more holistic ways of reporting on progress from the start, with an equal emphasis on actions, results, and lessons learned. Sharing regular progress on multiple measures, communicating insights about the reasons for that progress, and highlighting lessons learned through both success and failure requires vulnerability, but it is the kind of honesty that is needed from organizations that lead for racial justice. Most important, we believe that we should do more storytelling of empowered school communities, paint richer portraits of students of color who are striving and thriving, and highlight educators and teams who are learning to lead and teach in ways they never imagined possible. New leaders must take advantage of every opportunity to share new, and true, narratives about what is really happening in their schools and districts while lifting emergent learning. Every day brings an opportunity to speak the truth, share the learning, and stay focused on what is possible.

A SKILL: ADAPTIVE LEADERSHIP

Finally, we would like to share some skills to practice. Ronald Heifetz and Donald Laurie, in their now classic article on adaptive leadership, "The Work of Leadership," outline a set of leadership skills for practice that we believe are especially relevant for collaborative strategy development and action planning.[20] In table 8.1, we remind our readers of those practices and provide some related tips for equity-focused leadership entry with a focus on strategy.

TABLE 8.1 Tips for equity-focused strategy development

ADAPTIVE LEADERSHIP PRACTICES	TIPS FOR EQUITY-FOCUSED STRATEGY DEVELOPMENT
Get on the balcony Don't get swept up in the field of play. Instead, move back and forth between the "action" and the "balcony."	• Equip your strategy development team with the insight you've gathered from a broad range of voices, prioritizing the people closest to the daily work and the problems. • Be sure that this information includes themes that exist among nondominant groups. • Draw out stories from the data for the team so that they can zoom in and out, using specific examples to demonstrate implications for the larger strategy.
Identify your adaptive challenge Adaptive challenges are the murky, systemic problems with no easy answers. Solving them requires the involvement of people throughout your organization.	• Name the adaptive challenge(s) with your planning group. • Be explicit about challenges rooted in racism and oppression. • Involve students, families, and staff as you plan so that you can explore the problem and its root causes before moving to solutions.
Regulate distress To inspire change—without disabling people—pace adaptive work.	• As you plan, think about when and how the work will directly impact those working most closely with children or with the community your organization serves. • Consider with your team where the windows of opportunity exist for action. In other words, what seems most ripe for change? • Build into your strategy from the beginning ways to stay grounded in the "word on the street" as you implement.
Maintain disciplined attention Encourage managers to grapple with divisive issues, rather than indulging in scapegoating or denial.	• As you develop your strategy and action plan, talk about the ways of working that will be necessary to grapple with divisive issues, especially issues related to racism in all its forms. • Consider how to use/adapt existing venues, like regular team meetings, professional development time, and retreats, to pause, check in, and explore viewpoints.
Give the work back to employees Instill collective self-confidence—versus dependence on you—by supporting rather than controlling people.	• Strategy development doesn't require working out every action item in advance. Encourage your team members to make the work their own—adapt, innovate, and communicate. • Back up people when they make mistakes (unless they are egregious mistakes that do harm).

continued

TABLE 8.1 *Continued*

ADAPTIVE LEADERSHIP PRACTICES	TIPS FOR EQUITY-FOCUSED STRATEGY DEVELOPMENT
Protect leadership voices Don't silence whistleblowers, creative deviants, and others exposing contradictions within your organization.	• When you plan, provide space to talk about what will be hard, what could go wrong, and how you will learn from these inevitable challenges. • Agree on ongoing plans related to listening and learning. • Don't ignore the people who dissent, instead, listen to them. At the very least, they will provide you with clues as to why the change is hard.

Note: The first column represents Heifetz and Laurie's "Idea in Practice" as described in Ronald Heifetz and Donald L. Laurie, "The Work of Leadership," *Harvard Business Review*, December 2001, https://hbr.org/2001/12/the-work-of-leadership.

FINAL REFLECTION

When each of us looks back on our own work to develop strategy and put it into action, we are reminded of how reliant we were on all that we did during our leadership entry process which built the momentum for change. We simply couldn't have developed the strategy without the insight, shared understanding, and consensus building that we did in advance. We are also reminded that strategy development, as opposed to traditional strategic planning, isn't about delineating every possible action in advance. It is about developing a coherent set of strategy levers (or action areas) that hold together and represent a theory of how your actions will lead to the outcomes you desire. Most important, strategy development and action planning offer the opportunity to create ongoing routines for testing that theory and learning along the way alongside the people you serve.

As you plan for your leadership entry, consider these reflective questions:

- Who should be involved in strategy development and action planning? How will you authentically involve those who are most experiencing the problems in your organization?
- How will you use the process to create a more robust vision of success?
- How will you work with your team to identify the real problems that stand in the way of success?
- How will you coconstruct a coherent strategy that addresses those problems and realizes your vision, leaving room for learning along the way?
- How will you design the process so that it results in new behavior?

CHAPTER 9

SELF AND COMMUNAL CARE

As you grow older, you will discover that you have two hands,
one for helping yourself, the other for helping others.

—MAYA ANGELOU

Beginnings are ripe with opportunity and possibility, which is why careful planning of one's leadership entry is so important. Education leaders transitioning into a new role can present themselves again, shedding aspects of their leadership style they want to leave behind and amplifying the best parts of who they want to be. Leadership entry offers a natural opportunity to ask hard questions about the local context, explore different perspectives, and develop an understanding that unlocks powerful solutions. It can also lead to new trusting relationships that, when cultivated, motivate a community to act. If done with a focus on equity from the start, a leader is positioned to bring about transformational change. Despite all its promise, however, leadership entry is also precarious, which is why we emphasize self and communal care in the surrounding circle of our framework (see figure 9.1 and the "Theory of Action for Equity-Focused Leadership Entry" box).

In our empathy interviews with education leaders, some of whom entered their roles during the COVID-19 pandemic, the need for both individual and collective care and healing was unmistakable.[1] They shared with us that during leadership entry they often sensed that their communities were overwhelmed by the systemic problems they faced, problems rooted in racism and White supremacy and resulting in intergenerational poverty and violence. Their organizations often dealt with unresolved organizational and administrative

FIGURE 9.1 Entry for Equity Framework

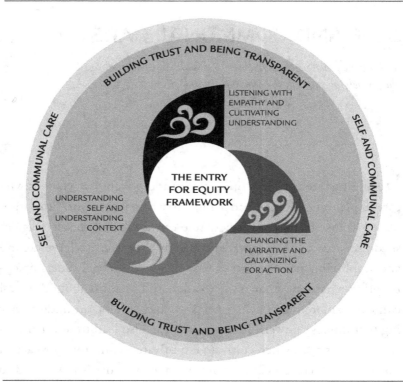

dysfunction, exacerbated by disruptive leadership turnover, which left people wounded. In many cases, the political environments they entered were toxic, riddled by battles between board members, unhealthy relationships with employee unions, and combative and defensive ways of working with the media. When a new leader steps in, much of this unresolved pain and suffering is unearthed and experienced anew.

While witnessing these community and organizational problems up close is crucial for effective leadership entry, it is challenging to bear emotionally. At the very least, it can leave a leader feeling drained at the end of the day, but it can also result in vicarious or secondary trauma.[2] And for some leaders, especially leaders of color,

THEORY OF ACTION FOR EQUITY-FOCUSED LEADERSHIP ENTRY

As described in chapter 1, our framework introduces eight critical dimensions that we believe leaders ought to consider in the design of their leadership entry. Taken together, these dimensions represent a theory of action, an "if . . . then . . . " statement that articulates the relationship between actions and outcomes.[a]

IF THE LEADER:

- looks inward to understand their multiple identities as well as outward to understand the social, cultural, and historical context of the community they serve;
- commits to transparency in the process, is explicit about issues related to racism and oppression from the beginning, and actively builds trust along the way;
- centers the voices of those who are most experiencing the problems, listens with empathy to multiple perspectives, and develops a shared and compassionate understanding of the organization's strengths, challenges, and opportunities;
- uses this shared understanding to tell an honest narrative about the organization that disrupts deficit thinking and racial stereotypes and galvanizes the community for collective action; and
- provides space for healing, self-care, and the care of others

then the leader is more likely to set in motion an equity-focused change effort that can lead to sustainable change. These eight dimensions, each interrelated, are essential for leaders who want to lead for equity from the beginning.

a. Stacey Childress, *Note on Strategy in Public Education*, PEL-011 (Cambridge, MA: Public Education Leadership Project at Harvard University, June 2004), https://projects.iq.harvard.edu/files/pelp/files/pel011p2_modified.pdf.

it can be retraumatizing. Holding the historical pain and suffering of a community is both a duty and a privilege, but it takes a toll. If that weren't enough, there is the added stress of being under more scrutiny as a new leader, a magnified reality for female leaders and leaders of color. We know that leaders of color, for example, often aren't trusted for their expertise, receive less support, and are subject to harsher criticism, especially when they are from out of town.[3] In one of our interviews, a new female superintendent of color who entered her role at the start of the COVID-19 pandemic shared how she was continually asked by her school board to reference experts and provide evidence to support her decision-making, while the White men in surrounding districts were simply trusted to do what was right. There is no actual honeymoon period in leadership entry, and the stress is real.

Ultimately, these compounding stressors can lead to adverse effects. Too many of the leaders we interviewed shared the damaging physical and psychological effects they experienced during their entry periods. One Black male superintendent shared that he got pneumonia during his first few months on the job. A Black female central office leader shared with us the constant anxiety she was feeling, worried that she would forget to do something that would get her or the school district in trouble. Another Latina school leader shared the sometimes debilitating challenges she faced with imposter syndrome during her entry period. According to therapist Resmaa Menakem, "When people experience repeated trauma, abuse, or high levels of stress for long stretches of time, a variety of stress hormones get secreted into their bloodstreams. In the short term, the purpose of these chemicals is to protect their bodies. But when the levels of these chemicals remain high over time, they can have toxic effects."[4]

We don't share this harsh reality to dissuade leaders from taking on education leadership roles. On the contrary, we share it because we believe that there is an opportunity to introduce healthier routines that foster healing, self-care, and care for others from the very start. There is a better way to do this work, and it begins with us. When leadership entry is reframed as more than an opportunity to learn and make positive change, but an opportunity for healing and care, it takes on profound proportions. Here, we share three final implications for leadership entry, focusing on routines that will help us sustain ourselves and our communities as we lead for racial equity.

MAKE TIME FOR HEALING

There is no question that education leaders who lead for racial justice will hear about, see, and experience the effects of trauma during their leadership entry, and in the United States, racial trauma is ubiquitous. Whether it is historical trauma, intergenerational trauma, institutionalized trauma, personal trauma, or secondary trauma, we all are victim to it no matter our race, individually and collectively, albeit at varying degrees.[5] As such, we believe it is essential to design one's leadership entry with a healing-centered approach that can lead to growth.[6]

According to Shawn Ginwright, who studies African American youth development, a healing-centered approach is about more than mitigating harm; it is about creating conditions for our collective well-being.[7] Using Ginwright's descriptors for healing-centered engagement, we draw out the implications for leadership entry.[8] Healing-centered engagement:

- *"Is explicitly political, rather than clinical."* In equity-focused leadership entry, a healing-centered approach ensures that those who have experienced collective trauma have the agency to change the conditions that produced the harm.
- *"Is culturally grounded and views healing as the restoration of identity."* In leadership entry, a healing-centered approach offers opportunities to process collectively in communities and with attention to race, ethnicity, and culture.
- *"Is asset driven and focuses on the well-being we want, rather than symptoms we want to suppress."* In leadership entry, conversations do not just focus on the problems and the harm, but on collective strengths and possibilities.

- *"Supports adult providers with their own healing."* Leadership entry is designed with the assumption that everyone deserves to be well, both the youth we serve and the adults who serve them.

At every turn during leadership entry, opportunities for healing exist—in one-on-one meetings, focus groups, and community forums, as well as in informal conversations that occur while in the community. Even the ways we communicate can foster healing, especially when we acknowledge hard things. But a leader can also build more intentional spaces for healing into their leadership entry approach, either proactively or in response to issues that arise, which can lead to positive change. While information from these intentional spaces for healing should not be used in the formal reports a new leader issues during leadership entry, we believe that creating intentional space for healing is essential for an organization and its community to thrive.

The Circle Process

One potential strategy to incorporate is the circle process. According to the Healing Justice Project, "Deriving from practices of Native Americans, First Nations, and Indigenous peoples, the Circle Process allows for the formation of relationships, the honoring of voices, and the creation of unity. The process is, at its essence, a story sharing process, which brings together people as equals to have open exchanges about difficult issues or painful experiences in an atmosphere of respect and concern for everyone."[9] The process, in which participants sit in a confidential circle and take turns speaking to prompts without interruption in rounds, fosters deep listening, shared responsibility, and personal transformation. We believe the process could be used proactively for new leaders during their listening and learning phase, with a focus on recognizing historical context and its relationship to present-day realities.

Affinity Groups

Another strategy to consider are racial affinity groups, sometimes called caucuses. Racial affinity groups provide an opportunity for people to make meaning and find purpose within their own racial or ethnic groups. In a recent landscape analysis commissioned by the Black Teacher Project, the author explains that racial affinity groups "can support . . . educators in understanding how they have been harmed by racial oppression, how to heal from that harm, how our systems are designed to perpetuate that oppression, and how their racial identity connects to what actions they can take to transform systems."[10] We believe that the use of affinity groups could be especially supportive during the sensemaking stage of leadership entry before action planning. Not only could the process lead to new insights, but it could provide space for emotional release and much-needed healing.

The Pause

While this is not a formal process, we want to emphasize that there is almost always time to pause, think, and feel, unless there is a crisis that requires immediate action. Better to slow down the decision-making process, for example, to explore alternative points of view and discuss root causes. Powering through to action, when unnecessary, can cause further harm. Especially when you are new to an organization, you deserve to give yourself a moment to think and feel your way through complexity. The opportunity to build shared understanding before moving forward can not only reduce harm but offer moments of healing.

MAKE TIME FOR SELF-CARE

Healing-centered sensemaking is critical, but equity-focused leaders need to take care of their minds, bodies, and souls too. The hard truth is that negative internal dialogue, unhealthy routines, and racing minds are often fueled by the people who are opposed to the changes we are pursuing. Self-care can be an act of resistance, and it is critical if we are going to make the transformative change students deserve.

Here are a few of the ideas shared with us during our conversations with leaders, all focused on redirecting some of our limited time to our well-being.

Positive Self-Talk

One of our interviewees said, "I would dedicate more time to telling myself—you are doing the best you can."[11] Our inner dialogue can either exacerbate the stress of our jobs or mitigate it. When we routinely blame ourselves, focus on the negative, expect the worst, or see things as dichotomous, we not only tell ourselves a story that isn't true, but we increase our stress. The problems we face are much more complex than that, and negative self-talk doesn't help.

We encourage new leaders to pay attention to that inner dialogue and reframe it if it is habitually negative. When faced with a difficult decision, move from worrying about who you will upset to how you will help others understand your reasoning. When you begin to doubt yourself because you are doing something you've never done before, think instead about all you will learn that will serve your organization in the future. When you start to ruminate on failure, think about the opportunity to teach people the power of calculated risk-taking. Positive affirmations seem to help too. One of the leaders we interviewed talked about posting quotes in highly visible places for daily inspiration that kept her grounded in her values.

Eat, Sleep, and Exercise

We know that this is obvious but taking physical care of ourselves cannot be an afterthought. As education leaders, we sometimes think we must sacrifice everything for work, but that approach isn't sustainable. When we make too many sacrifices, it shows up in unhealthy ways in our daily interactions, and we can't see the work through. The leaders we talked to suggested basic adjustments. We know that these can sometimes seem impossible given all that we have happening in our lives but consider the following:

- *Bring a lunch, have a stash of healthy food at work, and drink lots of water.* Not eating at work is not only bad for you, but it sends an unfortunate message to those who work with and for you, as if eating is a sign of weakness. When you can, eat food that you love.
- *Go to bed earlier.* We know that the day starts early in school district life, so get to bed at a decent hour. Sometimes domestic duties or additional work tasks can keep us up late, but consider leaving the dishes in the sink and the emails in the inbox and get the sleep you need. As an aside, don't email people late at night, which can trigger negative emotional responses. If you are a nighttime email writer, use the email scheduling feature so that people do not receive your messages until work hours.
- *Get some daily exercise.* Not everyone can make it to the gym, for obvious reasons, but take a fifteen-minute walk each day. Take the stairs. Or even consider scheduling a walking meeting, which can be a healthy alternative to more time sitting in the office.
- *Practice mindfulness.* Leaders may also want to consider investing in mindfulness practice to stay more present, attuned to the body, and centered. Simple things can make a big difference, like simply pausing between meetings to breathe, get some water, or take a short but slow, mindful walk down the hall. By making minor adjustments to your daily ways of working, you can give your community the full and deep attention they deserve.

- *Eliminate random scrolling through social media.* At the very least, monitor the amount of time you spend scrolling through it. Or limit it to topics and people that bring you joy and inspiration. If you are a high-profile leader, consider assigning someone to scan it for you to keep you informed, but not distracted in unhealthy ways.

Manage Your Time

For leaders in education, managing time is crucial for prioritizing the technical activities required to get the work done, and too many of the new leaders we interviewed shared how time management was a struggle. How and when you use your time should be targeted and specific to organizational priorities and your own well-being. If time management is done well, you can be both efficient and effective.

- *Set clear goals.* Your goals should ultimately drive how you spend your day, not your tasks. Goal setting is so much more than a list of things to do. When done well, it should ensure that you are doing the right work at the right time.
- *Prioritize tasks.* Prioritizing tasks will allow you to boil down your goals into reasonable action steps. These tasks should drive your daily activities and help you to prioritize what's important and what can be done later.
- *Organize yourself.* Utilize your calendar accordingly, working with your assistant, if you have one. Every minute of your work schedule should be intentional. Schedule quiet time at the start or end of each week to clarify your goals and priorities. Schedule email time so that you aren't distracted by it. Shorten one-on-one time where possible to become more efficient. Schedule office hours and be wary of open-door policies. And schedule longer blocks for deeper thinking and planning.[12]

No matter how you choose to manage your time, be sure to reflect on how its working for you. If necessary, reevaluate how you manage your time and create a strategy that will work best for you.

Remember You Are Not Alone

In April 2021, Reba Hodge, a Black vice principal in Syracuse, New York, wrote an opinion piece for *Education Week* called "The Year of Scourges: How I Survived Illness and Racism to Find My Tribe."[13] In the article, she explains that sustaining herself during her most challenging year as an educator required that, among other things, she find her people. She said, "I am quite selective about that group. The teachers are Black, of color, and white. The commonality among them is that they are committed to improving their own teaching practices as they work to create conditions where Black and brown students can thrive. My only essential is that these folks prioritize the health and overall well-being of our young people." She realized that finding her people, across racial and other identities, gave her the stamina she needed to continue. Leaders of color need to find their own spaces too. Doing so can provide a source of joy, wisdom, and power. And White equity-focused education leaders need to do the same, resisting the urge to act as a lone savior or to disassociate with other White colleagues. No one can do this work alone.

DEVELOP CARE HABITS FOR THE LONG HAUL

Finally, we know that real change—changing systems and institutions—takes time. There are windows of opportunity that allow us to move fast, and we should move quickly when those opportunities arise, but more often, the work is painfully slow. Even what looks like rapid change is usually built on imperceptible foundational shifts that occurred over time. The work of most leaders is not steering through the crisis, but sustaining commitment, modulating energy, and stewarding resources to be ready to take advantage of moments of radical transformation. This requires faith, or hope without evidence, that something better is possible. Establishing habits of care from the beginning will help you through the often slow process of change. Consider these questions as you begin to build routines that foster self-care and care of others from the beginning.

- *Daily.* What is the thing you can do each day, even for five minutes, to create space for joy, presence, or peace? Being present is essential for equity-focused leaders.
- *Weekly.* What matters to you beyond your work, and how can you create space for that every week? Staying tethered to what matters will give you the energy to keep going and set a great example for your team.
- *Quarterly.* What do you need to fully unplug for a long weekend? Establishing your boundaries and holding yourself to them both frees you to refuel and empowers those who work with you.
- *Yearly.* What does it look like to have an annual day of reflection to assess the alignment between your values, your organization's values, your actions, and your impact? Staying tethered to your values, your commitment to racial equity, and who you want to be in this work is essential.
- *Over your career.* How will you know when it is right to transition to the next role? What is best for the organization? And for you? Who can mentor and guide you in this decision? While this book is about beginnings, endings matter too, and your current leadership role has an end. We must grant ourselves permission to step into and out of the arena as our gifts match or mismatch with the moment and our energy.

A FINAL REFLECTION

When Jen started her superintendency, she spent twelve to fourteen hours at work each day. As a first-time female superintendent, she thought she had to be the most prepared person in the room. Of course, this set the tone for her leadership in the beginning, and it took a toll on her family. When Rodney started his first cabinet-level leadership role, he focused heavily on individual relationship building but found that he couldn't fully break through his outsider status, even with people who looked like him. As a result, he never quite found his people in this new community, outside of a few trusted colleagues grappling with the same dynamic. When Adam started his first principalship, he admits, he was trying every day simply to keep it together. But by doing so, he was protective of his vulnerabilities, and it was harder to build trust as a result.

We share this because we did all we were supposed to do in leadership entry, everything that we had been taught, and we did it well, but we didn't center the importance of healing, self-care, and care of others. It is, for us, the most important shift we have made to our leadership practice over time. As we became more humane leaders, to ourselves and to others, we found more joy, strength, and love for our work. The integration of family and work life became easier. Relationships became stronger. The bank of goodwill and trust was fuller. Mostly, we found that we no longer felt alone.

Education leaders who work with children and families tend to see up close startling examples of beauty, love, and generosity. These moments, often between teachers and students, make it all worthwhile. But we also witness the manifestations of oppression, some of them subtle, others blatant and ugly, all of which affect us personally, especially because these issues are hard to fix. When reframed, leadership entry presents an opportunity for healing and a chance to establish routines for self-care and the care of others from the very beginning. If done well, it will leave us whole, stronger, more resilient, and more capable of making the change our communities deserve.

LITERATURE ON ENTRY PLANNING

To inform our thinking on leadership entry, identify gaps, and pinpoint implications for our work, we looked at existing frameworks, sample entry plans, and written case studies. Ultimately, there were a few that rose to the top as the most informative. We share a summary of those here, in order of publication date, for anyone who seeks to explore the topic further. We found Barry Jentz's *Entry* and Peter Daly and Michael Watkins's *The First 90 Days in Government* to be especially useful, and we draw out their frameworks in tables A.1 and A.2.

EDUCATION SECTOR LEADERSHIP ENTRY

Barry Jentz with Joan Wofford, *Entry: How to Begin a Leadership Position Successfully* (Newton, MA: Leadership and Learning, 2008).

> This book provides many samples of entry plan materials, including letters and interview questions from school and district-level leaders.

Stacey M. Childress, Denis P. Doyle, and David A. Thomas, *Leading for Equity: The Pursuit of Excellence in the Montgomery County Public Schools* (Cambridge, MA: Harvard Education Press, 2009).

> This book takes a deep look at Jerry Weast's tenure as superintendent of the Montgomery County (Maryland) Public Schools and his efforts to address the implications of race and

class on student learning. It provides a detailed case study of how one leader managed change with significant attention to his leadership entry.

Sarah Fiarman, *Becoming a School Principal: Learning to Lead, Leading to Learn* (Cambridge, MA: Harvard Education Press, 2015).

This book delves deep into the specific challenges new principals face. It provides resources on data-informed leadership, addressing racial bias, building relationships, and sharing leadership.

Linda Chen, "An Entry Guide for Assistant Superintendents of Curriculum and Instruction in Urban School Districts: Starting Strong to Transform Learning, Teaching, and Leading" (PhD diss., Teachers College, Columbia University, 2016).

This dissertation is focused on entry for leaders in charge of curriculum and instruction. The appendix is full of tools and resources helpful for gathering data and sensemaking.

Douglas Reeves and Robert Eaker, *100-Day Leaders: Turning Short-Term Wins into Long-Term Success in Schools* (Bloomington, IN: Solution Tree Press, 2019).

This book provides insights into how to deliver on quick wins early in a role.

GENERAL LEADERSHIP ENTRY

Linda Hill, *Becoming a Manager: How New Managers Master the Challenges of Leadership* (Boston: Harvard Business School Press, 2003).

This seminal text in business schools explores the experiences of new managers and the nuances of transitioning into a management role.

Peter H. Daly and Michael Watkins with Cate Reavis, *The First 90 Days in Government: Critical Success Strategies for New Public Managers at All Levels* (Boston: Harvard Business School Press, 2006).

> This book takes the ideas of the original *First 90 Days* text and adapts them to the public sector. There are enhanced resources and reflective questions for those in roles where the political frame and working through governmental processes are critical.

Michael D. Watkins, *The First 90 Days: Proven Strategies for Getting Up to Speed Faster and Smarter, Updated and Expanded* (Boston: Harvard Business Review Press, 2013).

> This is another seminal text of business schools. It helped to launch intentional leadership entry as a common practice. There are resources for learning, developing strategy, and building teams from a private-sector business point of view.

Julie Zhuo, *The Making of a Manager: What to Do When Everyone Looks to You* (New York: Portfolio/Penguin, 2019).

> This book explores the technical skills of management for first-time leaders by using the author's experiences at Facebook. It includes ideas for building teams, feedback, hiring, and attending to culture.

Finally, we share two of the frameworks that we believe can complement the approach described in this book with additional tactical ways to enter well. Both are from books that are referenced in the list above.

In education, we highlight the work of Barry Jentz, who has been using his planned entry approach with leaders for about forty years. Each of us has used Jentz's planbook (*Entry: How to Begin a Leadership Position Successfully*) and recommended it to others. In it, Jentz warns that new leaders, struggling to meet high expectations and multiple demands ("hit the ground running") tend to rely on superficial data, act too quickly, and, in a word, fail. As an alternative, he suggests a "hit the ground learning" approach with attention to first understanding the organization as it is understood by its members, thus producing both trust and the collective, shared knowledge necessary to sustain and improve the organization. There are four key steps in the process that he posits will result in four outcomes: direction, trust, new thinking, and new behavior (see table A.1). This guidance, especially its focus on inquiry and collaborative sensemaking, has greatly influenced our thinking about effective leadership entry.

TABLE A.1 From *Entry: How to Begin a Leadership Position Successfully*

Step 1: Design entry plan	Direction	To demonstrate that decision-making and direction will follow collective inquiry, the new leader engages key people in designing and making public an entry plan that is transparent about the sequence of collaborative inquiry activities that will result in a blueprint for change.
Step 2: Generate data systematically	Trust	To generate trust, respect, and credibility, a new leader takes time to understand key people and the organization from the *inside out* before making decisions.
Step 3: Make sense of data	New Thinking	To produce collective new thinking and build consensus for entry plan findings, data must be shared and understood collectively.
Step 4: Form action plan	New Behavior	To produce decisions that will be implemented and positively reshape the organization, new thinking must be tested in the form of action planning and adjusted to ensure success.

Source: Barry Jentz with Joan Wofford, *Entry: How to Begin a Leadership Position Successfully* (Newton, MA: Leadership and Learning, 2012).

One of the most widely known books on leadership entry is Michael Watkins's *The First 90 Days*, which focuses on leadership entry in business. Watkins, with others, wrote a similar book of guidance tailored for government. Watkins notes in the government book that "transitions are critical times when small differences in your actions

can have disproportionate impacts on results." While there are nuanced differences between business and government, the frameworks
are similar. This practical guidance is something we have drawn on,
and each strategy represents a basic tenet of solid leadership entry
planning that we think resonates across sectors (see table A.2).

TABLE A.2 From *The First 90 Days in Government*

1	Clarify expectations	• Build a productive working relationship with your new boss • Understand his or her expectations • Understand and factor in the expectations of other key stakeholders • Plan for a series of critical conversations about the situation, expectations, style, resources, and your personal development
2	Match strategy to situation	• Diagnose the situation accurately • Determine challenges and opportunities • Develop your action plan
3	Accelerate learning	• Assess the organization's mission, services, technologies, systems and structures, culture, and politics • Decide systematically what you need to learn and how you will learn it most efficiently
4	Secure early wins	• Develop a set of goals—results to be achieved and behaviors to be changed—that you will accomplish by the end of your first year • Figure out where and how you will get early wins to build your credibility, create momentum, and lay the foundation for achieving your longer-term goals
5	Build the team	• Evaluate members of your team • Consider restructuring the team to better meet the demands of the situation
6	Create alliances	• Identify whose support is essential for your success and determine how to line those people up on your side • Cultivate internal and external supportive alliances
7	Achieve alignment	• Figure out whether the organization's strategy is sound • Bring its structure into alignment with its strategy • Develop the systems and skills necessary to realize strategic intent

continued

TABLE A.2 *Continued*

8	*Avoid predictable surprises*	• Understand the most common reasons why pre-dictable surprises happen • Take early actions to identify potential threats
9	*Manage yourself*	• Maintain your equilibrium and preserve your ability to make good judgments • Engage an advice-and-counsel network as an indispensable resource

Source: Peter H. Daly and Michael Watkins with Cate Reavis, *The First 90 Days in Government: Critical Success Strategies for New Public Managers at All Levels* (Boston: Harvard Business School Press, 2006).

MAJOR THEMES FROM EMPATHY INTERVIEWS

Over the past three years, we have interacted with several hundred leaders about their entry practices, their priorities when starting new roles, and the impact of using a structured entry process.

In design thinking, however, empathy interviews help the designer attain a more thorough understanding of potential problems before exploring and designing solutions. So to test our ideas and advance the framework development, we also engaged in a set of empathy interviews to better understand some of the nuances of leadership entry. We interviewed twenty school and school-district leaders who started a variety of school and district leadership roles in the last three years, making sure to choose leaders with different racial, ethnic, and gender identities. Each interview lasted about forty-five minutes and focused on the process they used, the resources they relied on, if any, the strengths and problems associated with their approaches, and the equity-focused issues that were most challenging.

Roles included: superintendent, executive director, assistant superintendent, director of diversity and inclusion, principal, assistant principal, and teacher leader.

We interviewed seven Black leaders, five Latinx leaders, six White leaders, two Asian leaders, ten female leaders (eight leaders of color), and ten male leaders (six leaders of color).

While the themes that emerged were largely confirming, there were subtle differences, often related to the leader's race and gender, role, and the circumstances around their hiring, that have added depth and nuance to each dimension of our framework. Below are the general themes that emerged:

Transparency Through Clear Public Phases

- Preentry provides time to gather data and gain insight from a select group
- A listen-and-learn approach provides opportunities to garner multiple perspectives and to seek understanding
- Action planning, which includes moving on some quick wins, builds credibility
- Regular reporting along the way and reporting back what you learned is key
- Each phase is important even during crisis, although the time frame might change
- Being transparent about decision-making is important from the start—the values you hold, the process you use, and the "why" behind the decisions that are ultimately made

Opportunity to Communicate Core Values

- Communicate your commitment to equity
- Take the opportunity to share your personal story
- Reflect on your identity

Deep Listening to Multiple Stakeholders

- Requires skills for managing conflict and making sense of different perspectives
- Include a combination of big meetings or forums, small groups, and individual conversations
- Get out into the community
- Interview direct reports to learn about the work already underway
- Do not assume people are too busy or don't care

Trust and Credibility Built Through Action/Follow-Through

- Show competence early on, especially in volatile contexts or during crisis
- Demonstrate that you have a double-track agenda—doing the job while also listening and learning
- Consider big and small opportunities to build trust

Healing/Self-Care

- Conversations had during entry unearth pain that is unresolved
- Times of crisis can amplify that pain
- For leaders of color, hearing some of these stories can be retraumatizing
- Self-doubt and imposter syndrome are common

TOOLS FOR EQUITY-FOCUSED LEADERSHIP ENTRY

In each chapter, we introduced at least one useful tool to support the design of leadership entry. Our goal in this appendix is to provide resources that you can return to as you design and put into motion your leadership entry plan. The tools are provided in order and with additional framing and details so that they can be used independently. It can be hard to pick up a book and try to recall in what chapter the resource you want is located—we hope this appendix makes it easier for you to find what you need.

INCLUDED TOOLS FOR EQUITY-FOCUSED LEADERSHIP ENTRY

- The Entry for Equity framework and phases
- Understanding Self: Leadership story development reflective questions
- Understanding Context: Mapping the landscape and equity-focused onboarding questions
- Building Trust and Being Transparent: Zaretta Hammond's trust generators and entry plan outline
- Listening with Empathy: Engagement strategies and Shane Safir's Mindful Listening tool
- Cultivating Understanding: The Cynefin framework and a problem categorization tool
- Changing the Narrative: Outline of an entry report
- Galvanizing for Action: Tips for equity-focused strategy development

THE ENTRY FOR EQUITY FRAMEWORK AND PHASES

Our framework (figure C.1) introduces eight dimensions that we believe leaders ought to consider in the design of their leadership entry, as shown in the graphic. It is designed to express the idea of building energy, movement, and power to produce change. In our experience, change is never linear, nor is leadership entry, but more like waves or wind, building momentum over time. Like waves, leadership entry is where small ripples can build over time into a powerful force. The framework also captures that every move we make as leaders should be done with trust building in mind and with care for both the people we serve and ourselves.

FIGURE C.1 Entry for Equity Framework

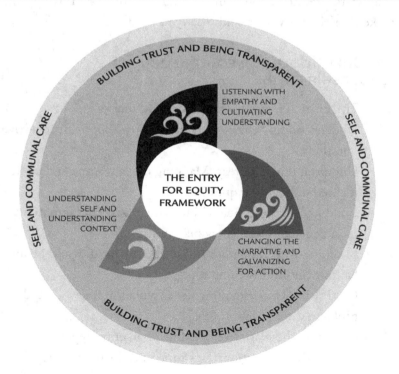

In addition to these framework dimensions, we suggest leaders plan their entry with a few typical phases in mind. These phases (and the suggested steps within) are shown in figure C.2. They do not have to be chronological—iteration is necessary, and sometimes steps happen simultaneously. It is also important to note that while leadership entry is often mapped out over the first ninety to one hundred days on the job, it can be shorter or longer depending on context. The key is transparency about your goals and process. Through every phase and step, no matter the order or the length of time, a leader is paying keen attention to themselves and their community's reactions, adjusting as they go.

FIGURE C.2 Leadership Entry Phases

PHASE 1 REFLECT	PHASE 2 LISTEN AND LEARN	PHASE 3 PLAN TO ACT
• Reflect on identity • Explore context • Gather available data	• Set goals and introduce yourself • Gather data through engagement • Share in sensemaking • Communicate	• Articulate shared vision • Identify root causes • Develop strategy • Commit to inquiry

UNDERSTANDING SELF: LEADERSHIP STORY DEVELOPMENT REFLECTIVE QUESTIONS

Purpose: This tool supports leaders as they reflect on their leadership identity. It allows leaders to lean into their strengths with new insights while helping to guard against blind spots that could impede their leadership.

Considerations for use: Set aside time to think about these questions, perhaps while walking or meditating. Spend thirty minutes capturing your thinking. Leaders can also share their responses for dialogue and further reflection when working with a coach, mentor, or colleague.

WHO AM I?
What personal or professional experiences contribute to who you are today?
What values did these experiences create?

WHY AM I HERE?
What personal connections can you make to the organization's mission/vision?
Why do you want to lead here, now?

WHAT CAN PEOPLE EXPECT FROM ME?
How does who you are and your reasons for taking the job affect the way you will lead? What is your approach to leadership?

UNDERSTANDING CONTEXT: MAPPING THE LANDSCAPE

Purpose: As you enter a new context, it is critical to understand how power is distributed. Not only is it important to identify early on who are the formal decision makers, but it is important to find out who their influencers are and begin to understand who might serve as both the champions for and the opposition to equity-focused change.

Considerations for use: These prompts can be answered independently as the leader learns more about the community they are joining. Leaders can also take these questions to their informal kitchen cabinet, the people knowledgeable about the community who are advising the leader as they enter their role.

QUESTIONS	ANSWERS (Be specific with actual names and titles)
Who is actively leading equity-focused change inside of your organization? Which of these people might serve as partners or guiding team members during your entry?	
Who is actively leading equity-focused work outside of your organization and in the larger community? Which of these people might serve as partners or guiding team members during your entry?	
Who are the decision makers in the organization? Who might need to be won over to make equity-focused change possible? Which of these people might serve as partners or guiding team members during your entry process?	
Who are the influencers in and outside the organization (including the influencers of decision makers)? Note that these are people who may not have positional authority. Which of these people might serve as partners or guiding team members during your entry process?	
Who are the people or groups who are most likely to experience loss with equity-focused change? Which of these people might serve as partners or guiding team members during your entry process?	
Who are the people or groups who will most likely actively oppose equity-focused change? Of these people or groups, who is most likely to engage meaningfully in discussion? Which of these people might serve as partners or guiding team members during your entry process?	

Source: This tool was adapted from the "Organizational Context and Authorizing Environment Assessment" as featured in the Harvard Graduate School of Education's Certificate in Advanced Education Leadership course on Driving Change.

UNDERSTANDING CONTEXT: EQUITY-FOCUSED ONBOARDING QUESTIONS

Purpose: Having a series of crucial conversations with your board, supervisor(s), and other key stakeholders, like key collaborators and colleagues, during the hiring process and extending through one's first weeks on the job, is key for shaping and clarifying expectations up front.

Considerations for use: Use these questions to guide critical conversations with your boss before and during the first weeks of your new role.

CONVERSATION	OBJECTIVE	SAMPLE EQUITY-FOCUSED QUESTIONS
Situation conversation	To gain understanding of how they see the state of the organization	How do racial inequality and other forms of oppression currently manifest in the organization? What ways of working have been put in place to identify and dismantle it?
Expectations conversation	To clarify and negotiate what you are expected to accomplish	To what extent can I be explicit about my focus on racial equity?
Style conversation	To discuss how you will interact and your preferred methods of communication and decision-making	What will it look like for me to manage "up" about crucial equity issues?
Resources conversation	To negotiate critical resources to do the job well	Are current resources aligned with our equity priorities? What resources can I expect if I am being asked to lead for equity?
Personal development conversation	To identify support focused on personal and professional growth	Where are the places I can find community? Where can I process safely and get support?
Anticipated resistance conversation	To openly discuss the ways that resistance will manifest in the organization	What will resistance look like, sound like, feel like? What support (and even protection) can I expect from you?

Note: The first five conversations come from Michael D. Watkins, *The First 90 Days: Proven Strategies for Getting Up to Speed Faster and Smarter, Updated and Expanded* (Boston: Harvard Business Review Press, 2013).

BUILDING TRUST AND BEING TRANSPARENT: ENTRY TRUST GENERATORS

Purpose: Trust does not happen by accident and new leaders need to build trust quickly. The following types of action and prompts allow leaders to determine how best they can build trust—especially when leading across difference.

Considerations for use: Select two or three questions below that you feel are most important to your ability to build trust with others. Answer the questions independently, or ask others what you might do that would be meaningful within your community. Commit to specific actions or routines and schedule them.

Entry Trust Generators

	ZARETTA HAMMOND'S TRUST GENERATORS	CONSIDERATIONS FOR THE DESIGN OF YOUR LEADERSHIP ENTRY
Proximity	People are more likely to build relationships with those whom they connect with across cultural levels. Engaging in what others value and mirroring their approach builds the connection on which the trust generators can begin.	As you design, consider: • How you will get close to the core work of your organization (e.g., through school visits or classroom observations) • How you will get close to the people who work in your organization (e.g., by walking the halls or eating lunch in the staff room) • How you will get close to the people you serve (e.g., by walking neighborhoods or taking public transportation) • How you will enter spaces where you might be an only or "other" of a salient identity with humility
Selective vulnerability	People respect and connect with others who share their own vulnerable moments. It means showing your imperfect human side.	As you design, consider: • How you might tell stories about yourself as a learner and about times when you struggled, and how those experiences inform your leadership • How you might talk about your experiences, successes, and failures working across differences, and how those experiences inform your leadership • How you will share what you are learning during your entry process for additional feedback • How you will own up to mistakes during your leadership entry and repair harm

continued

Entry Trust Generators, continued

	ZARETTA HAMMOND'S TRUST GENERATORS	CONSIDERATIONS FOR THE DESIGN OF YOUR LEADERSHIP ENTRY
Familiarity	People develop a sense of familiarity when they see someone often in a particular setting, such as at a bus stop every day or in the café on a regular basis.	As you design, consider: • How you will create predictable routines and stick with them (e.g., always have lunch in a school cafeteria or get coffee in the neighborhood where you know you'll run into people) • How you will post on social media or send communications in a predictable format • How you will consistently communicate updates on your entry and emerging themes
Similarity of interests	People create a bond with others who share similar likes, dislikes, hobbies, and so forth. This common affinity allows a point of connection beyond any obvious racial, class, or linguistic differences. This plants the seed of connection in the relationship.	As you design, consider: • How you will make personal connections (e.g., ask people about how they cultivate joy outside of work, or inquire about hobbies, family, and pets) • How to participate as a full member of your community and across communities (e.g., attend concerts, go to restaurants and movies, join a recreational sports club) • How to acknowledge and recognize local and national events and holidays that are significant to different groups within the community
Concern	People connect when others show concern for issues and events important to them, such as births, illnesses, or other life transitions. This plants the seed of personal regard.	As you design, consider: • How you will stay abreast of life and current events • How you will know to attend events that surface quickly in your community (e.g., demonstrations, memorials, vigils) • How you will recognize retirements or transitions that happen early in your entry before you fully build relationships
Competence	People tend to trust others who demonstrate they have the skill and knowledge, as well as the will, to help and support them. This plants the seed of confidence in others.	As you design, consider: • How you will share your entry plan and with whom • How you will track your promises and communicate when you deliver on them • How you will talk about race, gender, and sexual orientation and the impact of these topics on the work and on students, families, and staff. This includes demonstrating comfort with having candid conversations about race and privilege, especially if one is a White leader. • How you will name and interrupt patterns of inequity when you observe them during your entry process

Sources: Zaretta Hammond, *Culturally Responsive Teaching and the Brain: Promoting Authentic Engagement and Rigor Among Culturally and Linguistically Diverse Students* (Thousand Oaks, CA: Corwin, 2014); Karissa Thacker, *The Art of Authenticity: Tools to Become an Authentic Leader and Your Best Self* (Hoboken, NJ: John Wiley & Sons, 2016); *Culturally Responsive Leadership: A Framework For School & School System Leaders* (Long Island City, NY: Leadership Academy, 2020), https://www.leadershipacademy.org/wp-content/uploads/2020/09/Culturally-Responsive-Leadership-Actions-2020.pdf.

BUILDING TRUST AND BEING TRANSPARENT: SAMPLE ENTRY PLAN OUTLINE

Purpose: Leadership entry requires intentional design and preparation if it is to push against the status quo of inequity in most communities. Additionally, a written plan ensures both transparency and accountability for leadership. As a leader shares and then delivers on the plan, they build social capital on which they can launch more meaningful change efforts in the future.

Considerations for use: Take this outline to write your own plan. It can become a template in word processing or presentation software. It will be most effective when used in conjunction with the reflective planning tool in appendix D.

Introductory letter

- Introduce yourself (consider a video introduction that hooks the audience into reading the rest of the plan)
- Include a picture, if appropriate
- Consider a callout box with the goals for your entry process

Core values statements

- Describe why you are including them and how they drive the way you will enter your new position

Action steps

- List the data you will gather
- List the people and groups you will talk with and how, including the questions you will ask
- List any other actions that may need to be addressed right away, depending on context

Next steps

- Share what you will do to make sense out of the data you gathered

- Share how you will communicate what you learned
- If appropriate, share your plan for taking what you learned into strategy development and action planning

Conclusion

- Thank everyone
- Share how they can get involved
- Share contact info, if appropriate

LISTENING WITH EMPATHY: ENGAGEMENT STRATEGIES

Purpose: This framework and selection of tools provides leaders with ways to intentionally design for effective engagement with different audiences during the listening and learning phase of leadership entry. By attending to the categories of engagement, leaders can clarify their purpose and goals. When used in concert, these strategies can develop a system of robust engagement that results in opportunities to make positive change.

Considerations for use: Review the tips and tools to design your plan for listening and learning. Identify ways to disseminate information, gather input, and connect with your community that are aligned to a clear purpose and goals.

BUILDING BLOCKS OF ENGAGEMENT	IMPLICATIONS FOR ENTRY	TIPS AND TOOLS
Disseminating information	How you share opportunities for engagement and listening during your entry matters. Leaders should provide basic information about these opportunities with enough advance notice for people to attend. Leaders can also consider sharing critical information and questions in advance of the session and in multiple languages (if needed) to ensure that participants are prepared to engage.	Consider disseminating information: • On your website • Via social media • Via text/email • Through key personnel • Through key community leaders • In multiple languages

BUILDING BLOCKS OF ENGAGEMENT	IMPLICATIONS FOR ENTRY	TIPS AND TOOLS
Gathering input and data	During leadership entry, the leader should organize meetings (one-on-one, small group, and large group) to engage both a broad swath of people from within the organization and the community it serves and also more targeted focus groups. These meetings should be planned with accessibility in mind: interpretation/translation, childcare, transportation, evening or even weekend meetings, and food. There should be a plan for facilitation so that the leader can be fully present, and a plan for note-taking so that the leader can listen and take notes in a consistent form for data analysis.	Consider gathering input in multiple settings: • Staff meetings • School visits • Open community forums (virtual or in-person) • Key focus groups (e.g., Asian, Black, Indigenous, Latinx, youth, families, staff) • Key student groups (e.g., LGBTQ+, homeless, opportunity youth) • Advocacy groups (e.g., ELLs, special education, gifted and talented) • One-on-ones with key community leaders and elected officials
Discussing and connecting	In addition to these formal meetings, the new leader should seek out opportunities to listen in informal settings, taking advantage of every opportunity that comes their way. Those same questions can be woven into conversations over casual meals, community events, and coffee chats. Every interaction is an opportunity to collect more perspectives.	• Neighborhood center visits • Celebrations and community events • Meals • Coffee chats

Source: Tina Nabatchi and Matt Leighninger, *Public Participation for 21st Century Democracy* (San Francisco: Jossey-Bass, 2015).

LISTENING WITH EMPATHY: MINDFUL LISTENING TOOL

Purpose: This protocol will help you be fully present during your listening sessions. The goal is to show up in ways that are conducive to your own learning and the learning of others.

Considerations for use: Use this tool to prepare for your listening sessions and to debrief afterward. Ask trusted partners to attend the session and act as process observer using the graphic organizer to capture insights.

STEPS	NOTES AND REFLECTIONS
1. **Self-awareness.** Before the session, look into the mirror: • Who am I in this listening session through the lenses of race, culture, gender, age, and role? • What unconscious biases may be at work in my brain? • What messages might I be conveying, consciously or not? • What am I listening for?	
2. **Other awareness.** Stand in the other's shoes: • Who is the person/are the people in this listening session through the lenses of race, culture, gender, age, and role? • What unconscious biases may be at work in their brains? • What does the person/group seem to care about most in this listening session? • What are they listening for?	
Given all of this, how would you like to show up?	
3. **System awareness.** Look back on how the session went by stepping up on the balcony to analyze the various forces at play: • How would you describe the listening session? • What nonverbal behaviors stood out to you? • What indicators of trust did you see? Was there evidence of rapport, genuine listening, and mutual regard? • How were issues of identity, power, or bias at play? • Did the interaction reflect other patterns in the system? • What structural factors could be influencing it (e.g., time, place, protocol)?	
What are you learning that will have implications for future sessions? For follow-up items?	

Source: We reprinted, with permission, the Mindful Listening tool with slight modifications. The original tool can be found in its entirety in Shane Safir, *The Listening Leader: Creating the Conditions for Equitable School Transformation* (San Francisco: Jossey-Bass, 2017), and a printable version can be requested on Safir's website, shanesafir.com /resources.

CULTIVATING UNDERSTANDING: THE CYNEFIN FRAMEWORK AND A PROBLEM CATEGORIZATION TOOL

Purpose: Leaders must cultivate situational awareness to discern the kinds of challenges they face because problems in different types of contexts require unique responses. This tool can help a leader with that discernment process.

Considerations for use: Have your team use the characteristics below to categorize the organization's most pressing problems, and then use the tool to identify implications for communication and initial strategy.

Summary of the Cynefin framework

CONTEXT CHARACTERISTICS	APPROACH TO LEADERSHIP
Clear: Characterized by clear cause and effect relationships that are easily discernable by everyone.	A leader should sense, **categorize**, and then respond; apply "best" practices; rigid constraints exist.
Complicated: There exist multiple right answers, and though there is a clear relationship between cause and effect, not everyone can see it.	A leader should sense, **analyze**, and then respond; apply "good" practices; governing constraints exist.
Complex: Right answers do not exist, and there is no clear relationship between cause and effect; unpredictable.	A leader should **probe**, sense, and then respond; experiments lead to emergent practice; enabling constraints are needed to support innovation.
Chaotic: Searching for the right answer is pointless. The relationship between cause and effect is impossible to determine amid turbulence.	A leader should **act**, sense, and then respond; actions produce novel practice; there are no constraints.

Source: David J. Snowden and Mary E. Boone, "A Leader's Framework for Decision Making," Harvard Business Review, November 2007, https://hbr.org/2007/11/a-leaders-framework-for-decision -making; "Getting Started with Cynefin," (video), Cynefin Company, https://thecynefin.co/about -us/about-cynefin-framework/

Problem categorization tool

What are the big problems that have surfaced in your sensemaking?	What kind of problem is it (clear, complicated, complex, or chaotic) based on context? How do you know?	What are the implications for how you tell the data story to your community?

CHANGING THE NARRATIVE: OUTLINE OF AN ENTRY REPORT

Purpose: A formal entry report is typically five to fifteen pages, depending on the role, and it describes the entry process, summarizes the key insights and learning from entry, names potential priorities moving forward, and outlines the process for developing a strategy and action plan, if appropriate.

Considerations for use: This outline can be a starting place for building your own entry report. We encourage people to adjust for their own role and context. However, as each part is important, be intentional if you choose to delete a portion of the report. Be clear about why you are making the decision and interrogate your rationale for reasons such as limited time, hidden bias, or discomfort addressing issues of equity transparently.

Outline of an Entry Report

Letter of introduction and objectives of your entry plan:

- Reiterate your background, values, and reason for accepting the role.
- Articulate what equity means to you and the implications for your leadership.
- Reiterate the goals for your entry process. Articulate both what you hoped to learn and what you planned to accomplish through the process.

Methodology:

- Review the process used to engage with the organization during your entry period.
- Summarize the key actions you took and the information sources you explored as part of your learning.
- Provide the questions you asked during interviews that shaped your thinking.
- Share who helped you make sense of the data you gathered.

Strengths, challenges, opportunities, and emerging priorities:

- Celebrate the strengths and assets of the organization that are most relevant to future success.
- Highlight the major challenges and opportunities.
- List three to five major emerging priorities for the organization and your rationale for prioritizing them.

Next steps:

- If appropriate, share who you will be working with to develop a strategy to address the emerging priorities.
- Share when your community can expect to hear more.

Contact information:

- Share a way in which people can provide feedback on your entry report.
- Close with a note of gratitude and appreciation.

Design possibilities:

- Photos, links to videos, data displays, and icons can help to personalize your plan and ensure readers take away the most important information.
- Consider including quotes that inspire you, connect to your plan, or capture a key insight you heard from people during your entry process.
- Be clear about what you know and what you are still uncovering. Include essential questions and wonderings that will guide your work in the future.
- Name specific people and organizations who helped with the development of your entry report.

GALVANIZING FOR ACTION: TIPS FOR EQUITY-FOCUSED STRATEGY DEVELOPMENT

Purpose: Most change efforts are unsuccessful. These adaptive leadership practices increase the likelihood that a change effort will be adopted by a community. The tips below help pressure-test strategy development to both increase success and ensure that issues of equity are addressed through the strategy.

Considerations for use: These tips can be shared with the team that is charged with designing your strategy development process. Use them to design agendas so that no key practices are left out. They can also be used as criteria after the strategy development group convenes to evaluate their work and make revisions before sharing more broadly.

ADAPTIVE LEADERSHIP PRACTICES	TIPS FOR EQUITY-FOCUSED STRATEGY DEVELOPMENT
Get on the balcony Don't get swept up in the field of play. Instead, move back and forth between the "action" and the "balcony."	• Equip your strategy development team with the insight you've gathered from a broad range of voices, prioritizing the people closest to the daily work and the problems. • Be sure that this information includes themes that exist among nondominant groups. • Draw out stories from the data for the team so that they can zoom in and out, using specific examples to demonstrate implications for the larger strategy.
Identify your adaptive challenge Adaptive challenges are the murky, systemic problems with no easy answers. Solving them requires the involvement of people throughout your organization.	• Name the adaptive challenge(s) with your planning group. • Be explicit about challenges rooted in racism and oppression. • Involve students, families, and staff as you plan so that you can explore the problem and its root causes before moving to solutions.
Regulate distress To inspire change—without disabling people—pace adaptive work.	• As you plan, think about when and how the work will directly impact those working most closely with children or with the community your organization serves. • Consider with your team where the windows of opportunity exist for action. In other words, what seems most ripe for change? • Build into your strategy from the beginning ways to stay grounded in the "word on the street" as you implement.
Maintain disciplined attention Encourage managers to grapple with divisive issues, rather than indulging in scapegoating or denial.	• As you develop your strategy and action plan, talk about the ways of working that will be necessary to grapple with divisive issues, especially issues related to racism in all its forms. • Consider how to use/adapt existing venues, like regular team meetings, professional development time, and retreats, to pause, check in, and explore viewpoints.
Give the work back to employees Instill collective self-confidence—versus dependence on you—by supporting rather than controlling people.	• Strategy development doesn't require working out every action item in advance. Encourage your team members to make the work their own—adapt, innovate, and communicate. • Back up people when they make mistakes (unless they are egregious mistakes that do harm).

continued

Continued

ADAPTIVE LEADERSHIP PRACTICES	TIPS FOR EQUITY-FOCUSED STRATEGY DEVELOPMENT
Protect leadership voices Don't silence whistleblowers, creative deviants, and others exposing contradictions within your organization.	• When you plan, provide space to talk about what will be hard, what could go wrong, and how you will learn from these inevitable challenges. • Agree on ongoing plans related to listening and learning. • Don't ignore the people who dissent, instead, listen to them. At the very least, they will provide you with clues as to why the change is hard.

Note: The first column represents Heifetz and Laurie's "Idea in Practice" as described in Ronald Heifetz and Donald L. Laurie, "The Work of Leadership," *Harvard Business Review*, December 2001, https://hbr.org/2001/12/the-work-of-leadership.

REFLECTIVE PLANNING TOOL FOR EQUITY-FOCUSED LEADERSHIP ENTRY

This reflective planning tool supports and equips leaders for equity who begin new roles or initiatives or move to new organizational settings. Navigating through this tool will result in an equity-focused leadership plan that includes the following elements:

- Introductory letter with stated goals and core values
- Inquiry questions and a plan to gather data through engagement
- Approach to sensemaking
- Approach to communicating your findings
- Approach to action planning

All of this information can and should be included in your formal entry plan and can be shared with members of your community, as appropriate.

The reflective planning tool is organized into three distinct parts so that leaders can use the resources flexibly based on need.

Part I

The first table, below, is an overview of the typical phases and steps of a leadership entry process:

Step 0: Reflect on self and context
Step 1: Set goals and introduce yourself
Step 2: Gather data through engagement

Step 3: Share in sensemaking

Step 4: Communicate

Step 5: Plan to act

The table provides a summary of the key processes and deliverables associated with each step. It also provides the chapters you can review to learn more about that part of the process.

Part II

The largest part of the tool is a collection of detailed directions, activities, and graphic organizers to support leaders with completing every aspect of the entry process. These are organized with an overview, a set of criteria, the key deliverables, and detailed guidance for each protocol and process.

Part III

Finally, the tool ends with a recap of the criteria for each step that can be used for self-reflection or for providing feedback on an entry plan.

By exploring essential processes aligned with each step and by developing products, these deliverables support and equip leaders for equity as they begin new roles or initiatives, or as they transition into new organizational settings.

PART I: OVERVIEW

PHASES/STEPS	CHAPTERS TO REFER TO	PROCESSES TO EXPLORE	PRODUCTS TO DEVELOP AND DELIVERABLES
Phase I: Preentry			
Step 0: Reflect on self and context	Chapters 2–3, 9	• Understanding self-reflection • Understanding context reflection	• Key talking points

Phase 2: Listening and Learning			
Step 1: Set goals and introduce yourself	Chapter 4	• Core value identification • Goals for entry	• Entry letter • Entry goals and rationale
Step 2: Gather data through engagement	Chapter 5	• Big questions • Community engagement reflection	• Interview inquiry questions and protocol • Interview plan/calendar
Step 3: Share in sensemaking	Chapter 6	• Building understanding • Data organization summary • Sensemaking planning	• Data analysis process • Data overviews
Step 4: Communicate	Chapter 7	• Strengths-based language development • Communication method identification • Big message reflection	• Presentation and report • Analysis of deficit vs. strengths-based language
Phase 3: Action Planning			
Step 5: Plan to act	Chapter 8	• Preparation for inclusion of voices • Galvanize for action approach	• List of people involved in action planning • Description of product in action plan • Description of new community behaviors
Self and communal care throughout	Chapter 9	• Self and communal care reflections • Reflection commitments	• Scheduled care actions

PART II: COLLECTION OF DETAILED DIRECTIONS, ACTIVITIES, AND GRAPHIC ORGANIZERS

How to Use the Reflective Planning Tool

Each step starts with a set of criteria to focus your attention: authenticity, building trust, and communication equity. Think of these as the ABCs of your entry planning. A description of the "products to develop" clarifies the deliverables of each step. To support the creation of these deliverables, you may use any or all of the "processes to explore" before you work on the deliverables.

Step 0: Reflect on Self and Context

This initial step to your leadership entry often begins even before your official start date. It is essential to know who you are as a leader and learn as much as you can about the community you serve. It is helpful to reflect on your identity and role in relation to the local, historical, and community context. It is also a time to learn more about the organizational culture and examine the strengths and possible challenges through the lens of equity. We refer to this as *Step 0* because while you will begin your entry work here, you will also keep returning to it as you engage in the other steps and learn more about yourself and the context through the process.

CRITERIA	PRODUCTS TO DEVELOP AND DELIVERABLES
Authenticity The key talking points reveal more about the leader's identity *Building Trust* Questions shared about the new role and organization are grounded in inquiry, reality, and hope *Communicating Equity* The leader's talking points demonstrate equity mindsets and practices	*Key Talking Points:* Prepare your key talking points. These are the concepts, phrases, and stories you will use to share more about who you are and what you know about the organizational context and outcomes as you enter a new organization, role, and/or initiative.

Processes to Explore

Understanding self: Before you get started, consider how your racial identity and your other identities, including your personal and professional experiences, influence your leadership. This reflection will inform how you approach your introduction to the community you serve.

What about your identity gives you strength?	What may provoke fear, worry, or hesitation?	How might you be perceived?

Understanding context: Just like you need to be aware of how your own identity influences your leadership, you also need to be grounded in your local context. What do you know about the organization you will be serving and the community in which it is situated? What is the historical context? What are the top-of-mind present-day challenges and the connection between the two?

Who you will be serving	
Historical context	
Present-day opportunities and challenges	
What you are curious about	

Develop key talking points

What would you most like to share with your community from the ideas listed above?

Step 1: Set Goals and Introduce Yourself

The first step in developing a formal leadership entry plan is crafting an introduction to your community, a statement of your core values, and an articulation of your goals. It is important that this process happens with attention to your own identity, with trust building, and with an explicit focus on equity.

CRITERIA	PRODUCTS TO DEVELOP AND DELIVERABLES
Authenticity The introductory letter communicates an authentic picture of the leader **Building Trust** The purpose and goals of the entry plan are clear and considerate of trust building **Communicating Equity** The leader's list of values is clear and connected to beliefs about equity	Entry Letter: Craft a letter of introduction that shares something about yourself, your core values, and your goals for entry. Every step of the entry process builds or diminishes trust, so be sure to consider how you might begin that trust-building process here. And please know that you may draft slightly different versions of this letter for different audiences. Keep it to a page or less. If it is a video, try to stay within two minutes. Entry Goals and Rationale: It is important to articulate clear goals for your leadership entry period. Keep in mind that these goals may touch on relationship building and trust building as well as understanding the strengths and challenges of the organization. What do you want to learn? What do you want to accomplish?

Processes to Explore

Identify core values: Identify two to five one-word beliefs that are most important to you and that center your purpose with a focus on equity. These core values demonstrate what your community can expect of you, especially when faced with difficult decisions. Feel free to get creative here, and brainstorm before narrowing to the core values that are most meaningful for you.

Core Value	Write a sentence that describes the core value and why it is important to you.

Goals for entry: It is important to articulate clear goals for your leadership entry period. Keep in mind that these goals may touch on relationship building and trust building as well as understanding the strengths and challenges of the organization.

Entry Goal	Why does this goal matter to you? Why should it matter to other community members?	What are the equity implications?
Example: To identify the most pressing issues facing the organization.	*Example: My guess is that at least some of these issues will be long-standing issues that have been hard to budge. Exploring these issues and their root causes will help us identify our priorities.*	*Example: It is important that the most pressing issues represent real problems as described by those who are experiencing them. Telling stories about these issues could be a powerful way to mobilize collective responsibility and action.*

Step 2: Gather Data Through Engagement

Once you've thought about your introduction, the core values you want to express, and the goals you want to accomplish, the second step is to consider what questions you have and how you will gather data and information to answer those questions, including qualitative data gathered through engagement. It is important that this process is informed by your emerging understanding of the organizational context and its history.

CRITERIA	PRODUCTS TO DEVELOP AND DELIVERABLES

Authenticity
The leader models authentic inquiry and humility
 	
Building Trust
The leader makes transparent what they are doing and why
 	
Communicating Equity
The leader explicitly privileges the experiences of those at the margins
	Interview Inquiry Questions and Protocol:
	
	    Draft a set of questions to ask everyone you interview. Determine how you will share these questions in advance, before meeting with members of the community. Your protocol will likely include three to five inquiry questions that will drive your learning process, the key data sources you will review, and a list of the groups you will engage.
	
	Interview Plan/Calendar:
	
	    Develop a public calendar to share who you will speak to and when.

Processes to Explore

Big questions: What are the three to five questions you must be able to answer by the end of the entry process? What questions will help you gain insight into the organization's past, present, and possible futures? You can then consider what probing questions might help surface some of the nuances.

Three to five big questions	Possible probing questions on technical nuances: structures, patterns, and processes	Possible probing questions on relational nuances: relationships, identity, and information	Possible probing questions on environmental nuances: systems of advantage, oppression, and equity/social justice
Example: What are the organization's biggest strengths to build from?	*Example: What seems to work about reporting structures, collaborative planning, accountability systems, or decision-making processes?*	*Example: Where are trusting relationships strong? When does information flow well? Where/when do you feel "seen" and "heard"?*	*Example: What is the history of racial and social justice leadership in this organization/community? Who has led this work? What can we build on?*

For each of your big questions, what written or recorded media exist that can inform your learning? What else might you need?

Big question	Relevant documents and reports that exist	Reports or data summaries you might request and when

Community engagement reflection: Consider who you will engage to answer your three to five big questions, with a focus on seeking out voices that are most marginalized. It is okay to have some unique questions depending on the audience. You may also want to jot down some initial ideas about how best to engage each group in a way that fosters collective inquiry, learning, and trust.

Person, team, or community group	Specific questions to ask this person, team, or group	Logistics to design
		Examples: group size, where to meet, how long to meet, frequency of meetings required, invitation how and from whom, facilitation/note-taking, creating space for emotion, conflict, and relationship building

Step 3: Share in Sensemaking

Once you have gathered your data, you must determine how to make sense of all that you have collected, and the way you make meaning of your data must be intentional. Your goal as a leader is to develop a compassionate understanding of the organization and the community it serves.

CRITERIA	PRODUCTS TO DEVELOP AND DELIVERABLES
Authenticity The leader models the importance of checking for personal bias in the sensemaking process	Data Analysis Process: Build into your formal entry plan a description of who might be involved in sensemaking and how the process of analysis will be equity-focused.
Building Trust The leader includes the voices and perspectives of those at the margins and closest to the work	Data Overviews: You will create several visual displays that capture equity issues in a way that can leverage compassionate understanding toward community change (charts, infographics, photos). Consider how you might make different versions of your data displays based on the audience. Develop processes for revising your data displays as you learn from additional people and your thinking evolves.
Communicating Equity The process stays focused on identifying and understanding real problems and their root causes	

Processes to Explore

Building understanding: Exercising empathy and leaning into understanding of the individuals and collective community is an important starting point to make sense of data.

> **Think of an experience when you've had to advocate on behalf of someone. How did data help or hinder this process? How does this affect the way you might gather and understand data in your next context?**

Data organization summary: Consider how you will focus and organize the data you have gathered to make sense from it and develop a compassionate understanding of the organization and community you serve. Discernment is key. Narrow to only the most important sources. Be sure to consider in-group analyses, growth data, and coding of qualitative data so that the voices and perspectives of key groups (like students of color) are not buried.

Key data source	Method of analysis and/or possible data visualization ideas

Sensemaking planning: Determine who should analyze the data with you and what process you will use. Ensure that the people represented in the data are a part of the process.

Insert your participant list below:

Jot down ideas about protocols and processes, building on approaches to data analysis that might already be in use in your organization.	Consider new approaches that monitor for bias and humanize the data you are reviewing.

Step 4: Communicate

After you have made sense of that data, it is time to share what you have learned in a way that fosters reflection, inspires collective action, and changes the narrative, if needed. This is your chance to share a summary of what you think you have learned and the implications for the organization you serve.

CRITERIA	PRODUCTS TO DEVELOP AND DELIVERABLES
Authenticity The leader expresses respect for the organization, understanding of its community, and enthusiasm about the future	Presentation and Report: Summarize and share what you think you have learned and the implications for the organization you serve. Build into your formal entry plan a description of how you will communicate your findings and by when.
Building Trust The leader transparently shares information using the audience's preferred communication methods and is open to additional feedback	Analysis of Deficit vs. Strengths-Based Language:
Communicating Equity The leader demonstrates a clear call to action that is driven by the community, especially those most experiencing the problems; the leader's communication is positive, affirming, human-centered, and aspirational	Create a list of words and phrases that may deter equity-focused change. How might you disrupt deficit thinking, language, and perceptions in your communication every step of the way as a leader? Identify and make explicit words that leverage equity in the organization.

Processes to Explore

Strengths-based language development: Before you consider how best to communicate what you've learned, reflect on the language you've heard in the field that perpetuates negative narratives, deficit thinking, or stereotypes, perhaps especially about students of color and their families. How might you disrupt deficit thinking, language, and perceptions in your communication every step of the way as a leader?

Deficit language What language do you want to shed?	Strengths-based language What language do you want to embrace?

Communication method identification: Describe your methods for communicating what you've learned, including strengths, challenges, opportunities, and calls to action. Consider multiple modalities for sharing the message in order to be inclusive. Remember to use stories to give voice to what you've heard. Design an approach that provides additional feedback opportunities in order to test and revise your analysis.

Methods of sharing learning	Additional feedback opportunities

Big message reflection: What might be a few of the top-line messages you want to incorporate into your communications plan? You won't know for sure what the specifics are until you've finished the process, but you should anticipate stating something about the organization's many strengths, its biggest challenges, the opportunities that lie ahead, and a call to action.

Identify and describe your big messages:
1.
2.
3.

Step 5: Plan to Act

For some, creating an action plan based on your findings is the next logical step, and it may even be critical for building credibility as a leader. For others, it is not. You may be inheriting a plan that cannot yet be revisited in its entirety. Either way, it is important to think about how to use your entry process to galvanize for action. Knowing how to connect, inspire, and spur others toward increased leadership for equity is an integral part of leadership entry that can form the foundation for years to come.

CRITERIA	PRODUCTS TO DEVELOP AND DELIVERABLES
Authenticity The approach to action planning builds on natural momentum created during the entry process, with no predetermined outcome *Building Trust* The approach brings new people to the table who can provide insight into the design of solutions *Communicating Equity* The process and goals reflect the leader's commitment to equity	List of People and Groups Involved in Action Planning: List who will be involved in action planning. Be sure to include the core leadership team and those responsible for executing the strategy. Consider how students, parents, and community members can be included, especially those who have historically not been invited to the table. Description of Product in Action Plan: Cocreate a plan of action toward an equity change with community members. Keep in mind that these goals may touch on relationship building and trust building as well as understanding the strengths and challenges of the organization. What does the community want to accomplish? Description of New Community Behaviors: What are community members hoping to change in terms of new behaviors? Capture their requests and explicitly name these behaviors.

Processes to Explore

Preparation for inclusion of voices: List who will be involved in action planning. Be sure to include the core leadership team and those responsible for executing the strategy. Consider how students, parents, and community members can be included, especially those who have historically not been invited to the table.

List of voices to include:

Action planning approach: Cocreate with community members a plan of action toward equity-focused change in the organization and describe the timeline and hopes for new behaviors that are grounded in justice and action.

Describe the product that will hold the action plan.	What is the timeline, and how will the product be used?

Describe the new behaviors the community hopes to see through the development of the equity-focused action plan.

Closing Reflections

Self and Communal Care

Leadership entry is often such a busy time that self-care becomes an afterthought. Equity-focused leaders, however, recognize that leadership entry done well surfaces unresolved pain, and that hearing painful stories can be retraumatizing for the leader, too, especially leaders of color. Anticipating the time and space necessary to hold and process these conversations, and to make room for emotion, is critical for everyone, including the leader. The act of listening, sensemaking, and action planning, however, can produce healing if done with love, care, and compassion.

What ongoing structures will I put in place to exercise self-care?

What structures will I put in place to ensure that my leadership causes no harm, especially to those who have been historically harmed the most? What specific actions will bring healing to the community?

Ongoing Modes of Reflection

The practice of reflection inherent to leadership entry doesn't end in ninety or a hundred days. It is ongoing—and it's important to have structures for reflection to examine your leadership, your organizational context, and your progress, with attention to inquiry, learning, and equity throughout your tenure as a leader. Below, jot down a few ways of working that you will hold onto that you may also want to communicate to a larger audience.

Structures for self-reflection	Structures for reflection with others

PART III: CRITERIA FOR EACH STEP

On the next page is a summary of the criteria embedded in the reflective planning tool. When using the tool, consider the extent to which your comprehensive plan demonstrates a collective inquiry approach, a learning stance, and a focus on equity.

	Authenticity	Building Trust	Communicating Equity
Step 0: Reflect on Self and Context	The key talking points reveal more about the leader's identity	Questions shared about the new role and organization are grounded in inquiry, reality, and hope	The leader's talking points demonstrate equity mindsets and practices
Step 1: Set Goals and Introduce Yourself	The introductory letter communicates an authentic picture of the leader	The purpose and goals of the entry plan are clear and considerate of trust building	The leader's list of values is clear and connected to beliefs about equity
Step 2: Gather Data Through Engagement	The leader models authentic inquiry and humility	The leader makes transparent what they are doing and why	The leader explicitly privileges the experiences of those at the margins
Step 3: Share in Sensemaking	The leader models the importance of checking for personal bias in the sensemaking process	The leader includes the voices and perspectives of those at the margins and closest to the work	The process stays focused on identifying and understanding real problems and their root causes
Step 4: Communicate	The leader expresses respect for the organization, understanding of its community, and enthusiasm about the future	The leader transparently shares information using the audience's preferred communication methods and is open to additional feedback	The leader demonstrates a clear call to action that is driven by the community, especially those most experiencing the problems; the leader's communication is positive, affirming, human-centered, and aspirational
Step 5: Plan to Act	The approach to action planning builds on natural momentum created during the entry process, with no predetermined outcome	The approach brings new people to the table who can provide insight into the design of solutions	The process and goals reflect the leader's commitment to equity

NOTES

INTRODUCTION

1. In alignment with the National Association of Black Journalists June 2020 "Statement on Capitalizing Black and Other Racial Identifiers," we have decided to capitalize colors when they are used to describe race, including Black, White, and Brown, https://www.nabj.org/news/512370/NABJ-Statement-on-Capitalizing-Black-and-Other-Racial-Identifiers.htm. This editorial choice recognizes the racialization of every American. To read more, we recommend Nell Irvin Painter, "Why 'White' Should Be Capitalized, Too," *Washington Post*, July 22, 2020, https://www.washingtonpost.com/opinions/2020/07/22/why-white-should-be-capitalized/.

2. Muhammad A. Khalifa, Mark Anthony Gooden, and James Earl Davis, "Culturally Responsive School Leadership: A Synthesis of the Literature," *Review of Educational Research* 86, no. 4 (December 2016): 1272–1311, doi: 10.3102/0034654316630383 In this article, "minoritized" students are described as "individuals from racially oppressed communities that have been marginalized—both legally and discursively—because of their non-dominant race, ethnicity, religion, language, or citizenship."

3. Barry Jentz and Jerome Murphy, "Starting Confused: How Leaders Start When They Don't Know Where to Start," *Phi Delta Kappan* 86, no. 10 (June 2005): 736–44, doi: 10.1177/003172170508601005; Peter H. Daly and Michael Watkins with Cate Reavis, *The First 90 Days in Government: Critical Success Strategies for New Public Managers at All Levels* (Boston: Harvard Business School Press, 2006); Barry Jentz with Joan Wofford, *Entry: How to Begin a Leadership Position Successfully* (Newton, MA: Leadership and Learning, 2012); Michael D. Watkins, *The First 90 Days: Proven Strategies for Getting Up to Speed Faster and Smarter, Updated and Expanded* (Boston: Harvard Business Review Press, 2013).

4. *Hire Expectations: Big District Superintendents Stay in Their Jobs Longer Than We Think* (New Haven, CT: Broad Center, May 2018).

5. Stephanie Levin and Kathryn Bradley, *Understanding and Addressing Principal Turnover: A Review of the Research* (Reston, VA: National Association of Secondary School Principals, 2019).

6. Mim Carlson and Margaret Donohoe, *The Executive Director's Guide to Thriving as a Nonprofit Leader,* 2nd ed. (San Francisco: Jossey-Bass, 2010).

7. Gianpiero Petriglieri, "The Psychology Behind Effective Crisis Leadership," *Harvard Business Review,* April 2020, https://hbr.org/2020/04/the-psychology-behind-effective-crisis-leadership.

8. Linda Darling-Hammond, "A New 'New Deal' for Education: Top Policy Moves for States in the COVID 2.0 Era," *Forbes,* May 19, 2020, https://www.forbes.com/sites/lindadarlinghammond/2020/05/19/a-new-new-deal-for-education-top-10-policy-moves-for-states-in-the-covid-20-era.

9. Stephen Sawchuk, "Has COVID-19 Led to a Mass Exodus of Superintendents?," *Education Week,* May 6, 2021, https://www.edweek.org/leadership/has-covid-19-led-to-a-mass-exodus-of-superintendents/2021/05; Joe Heim and Valerie Strauss, "As Difficult School Year Ends, School Superintendents Are Opting Out," *Washington Post,* June 20, 2021, https://www.washingtonpost.com/education/superintendents-quit-pandemic-school-year/2021/06/19/e9e02594-cfaa-11eb-8014-2f3926ca24d9_story.html; Carl A. Cohn, "An Impossible Position," *School Administrator,* September 2021, http://my.aasa.org/AASA/Resources/SAMag/2021/Sep21/Cohn.aspx.

10. Ibram X. Kendi, *How to Be an Antiracist* (New York: One World, 2019).

11. Glenn Singleton, *Courageous Conversations About Race: A Field Guide for Achieving Equity in Schools* (Thousand Oaks, CA: Corwin, 2014).

12. David J. Snowden and Mary E. Boone, "A Leader's Framework for Decision Making," *Harvard Business Review,* November 2007, https://hbr.org/2007/11/a-leaders-framework-for-decision-making.

13. Snowden and Boone.

14. Chip Heath and Dan Heath, *The Power of Moments: Why Certain Experiences Have Extraordinary Impact* (New York: Simon and Schuster, 2017).

15. In Chicago Public Schools, the Local School Council is a school-based, locally elected body composed of parents, community members, school staff, and students (at the high school level). The council is responsible for approving the school's improvement plan and associated budget, as well as for the selection, evaluation, and renewal of the school principal.

16. Jentz, *Entry.*

17. Because leadership entry begins with the design of a process, we have drawn on the field of design thinking to fuel our approach, including resources from the Stanford d.school, the National Equity Project, and equityXdesign.

18. Elena Aguilar, *Coaching for Equity: Conversations That Change Practice* (San Francisco: Jossey-Bass, 2020).

CHAPTER 1

1. Stacey Childress, *Note on Strategy in Public Education,* PEL-011 (Cambridge, MA: Public Education Leadership Project at Harvard University, June 2004), https://projects.iq.harvard.edu/files/pelp/files/pel011p2_modified.pdf.

2. Beverly Daniel Tatum, *Why Are All the Black Kids Sitting Together in the Cafeteria?: And Other Conversations About Race* (New York: Basic Books, 2017), 99–110.

3. "Racism and Inequity Are Products of Design. They Can Be Redesigned," equityXdesign, November 15, 2016, https://medium.com/equity-design/racism-and-inequity-are-products-of-design-they-can-be-redesigned-12188363cc6a.

4. Anthony S. Bryk and Barbara Schneider, "Trust in Schools: A Core Resource for School Reform," *Educational Leadership* 60, no. 6 (March 2003): 40–44.

5. The Six Circle Model was originally developed by Margaret Wheatley and further refined by Tim Dalmau and Richard Knowles. It represents the technical and relational ways of working that define an organization's culture. We reference some of the components of this framework here.

6. Ivory A. Toldson, *No BS (Bad Stats): Black People Need People Who Believe in Black People Enough Not to Believe Every Bad Thing They Hear About Black People* (Boston: Brill Sense, 2019), doi: 10.1163/9789004397040.

7. Kim Scott, *Radical Candor: How to Get What You Want by Saying What You Mean* (New York: St. Martin's Press, 2017).

8. "Racism and Inequity Are Products of Design."

9. Resmaa Menakem, *My Grandmother's Hands: Racialized Trauma and the Pathway to Mending Our Hearts and Bodies* (Las Vegas: Central Recovery Press, 2017); Tracey A. Benson and Sarah E. Fiarman, *Unconscious Bias in Schools: A Developmental Approach to Exploring Race and Racism* (Cambridge, MA: Harvard Education Press, 2020).

10. Barry Jentz with Joan Wofford, *Entry: How to Begin a Leadership Position Successfully* (Newton, MA: Leadership and Learning, 2012); Matthew King and Irwin Blumer, "A Good Start," *Phi Delta Kappan* 81, no. 5 (January 2000): 356–60, https://www.jstor.org/stable/20439664; Robert O. Neely, William Berube, and Jerry Wilson, "The Entry Plan," *School Administrator* 59, no. 9 (October 2002).

11. Anthony S. Bryk et al., *Learning to Improve: How America's Schools Can Get Better at Getting Better* (Cambridge, MA: Harvard Education Press, 2015).

CHAPTER 2

1. All empathy interviews were conducted in confidentiality, and the names of interviewees are withheld.

2. Beverly Daniel Tatum, *Why Are All the Black Kids Sitting Together in the Cafeteria?: And Other Conversations About Race* (New York: Basic Books, 2017).

3. Tatum.

4. Muhammad A. Khalifa, Mark Anthony Gooden, and James Earl Davis, "Culturally Responsive School Leadership: A Synthesis of the Literature," *Review of Educational Research* 86, no. 4 (December 2016): 1272–1311, doi: 10.3102/0034654316630383.

5. Ronald A. Heifetz and Marty Linsky, "When Leadership Spells Danger," *Education Leadership* 61, no. 7 (April 2004): 36, https://www.ascd.org/el/articles/when-leadership-spells-danger.

6. "*Liberatory Design,*" http://www.liberatorydesign.com.

7. The entire Liberatory Design Card Deck can be found at https://static1.square space.com/static/60380011d63f16013f7cc4c2/t/60b698f388fe142f91f6b345/162 2579446226/Liberatory+Design+Deck_June_2021.pdf.

8. Liberatory Design Card Deck.

9. Liberatory Design Card Deck.

10. "Power," US English dictionary, Lexico, https://www.lexico.com/en/definition/power.

11. Liberatory Design Card Deck.

12. "The Lens of Systemic Oppression," National Equity Project, https://www.national equityproject.org/frameworks/lens-of-systemic-oppression.

13. Robin DiAngelo, "Antiracist Education and the Road Ahead," *Counterpoints* 398 (2012): 291, http://www.jstor.org/stable/42981496.

14. Kevin L. Nadal et al., "The Legacies of Systemic and Internalized Oppression: Experiences of Microaggressions, Impostor Phenomenon, and Stereotype Threat on Historically Marginalized Groups," *New Ideas in Psychology* 63 (December 2021), doi: 10.1016/j.newideapsych.2021.100895.

15. Vann R. Newkirk II, "The Language of White Supremacy," *The Atlantic,* October 6, 2017.

16. Nancy Gutiérrez (president and CEO, Leadership Academy) in discussion with the author, March 2021.

17. After our initial introduction of the leader in each chapter, we have chosen to refer to them by their first names to signal to our reader that we are all colleagues learning about leadership together.

18. Aysa Gray, "The Bias of 'Professionalism' Standards," *Stanford Social Innovation Review,* June 4, 2019, doi: 10.48558/TDWC-4756.

19. Jay M. Jackman and Myra H. Strober, "Fear of Feedback," *Harvard Business Review,* April 2003, https://hbr.org/2003/04/fear-of-feedback.

20. Marshall Goldsmith, "Feed Forward: Leadership Excellence," January 22, 2007, https://marshallgoldsmith.com/articles/1438.

21. Sylvia Ann Hewlett, "Cracking the Code That Stalls People of Color," *Harvard Business Review,* January 2014, https://hbr.org/2014/01/cracking-the-code-that-stalls-multicultural-professionals.

CHAPTER 3

1. All empathy interviews were conducted in confidentiality, and the names of interviewees are withheld.

2. "Context," Merriam-Webster.com dictionary, Merriam-Webster, https://www.merriam-webster.com/dictionary/context.

3. Rachel Roegman, "How Contexts Matter: A Framework for Understanding the Role of Contexts in Equity-Focused Educational Leadership," *Journal of School Leadership* 27, no. 1 (January 2017): 6–30, doi: 10.1177/105268461702700101.

4. Roegman, 10–12.

5. Roegman, 12–13.

6. Roegman, 13–15.

7. Roegman, 9–10.

8. "Racism and Inequity Are Products of Design. They Can Be Redesigned," equity Xdesign, November 15, 2016, https://medium.com/equity-design/racism-and -inequity-are-products-of-design-they-can-be-redesigned-12188363cc6a.

9. Paul Bredeson, Hans Klar, and Olof Johansson, "Context-Responsive Leadership: Examining Superintendent Leadership in Context," *Education Policy Analysis Archives* 19, no. 18 (June 2011), doi: 10.14507/epaa.v19n18.2011.

10. Eyder Peralta, "Timeline: What We Know About the Freddie Gray Arrest," The Two-Way blog, NPR, May 1, 2015, https://www.npr.org/sections/thetwo-way /2015/05/01/403629104/baltimore-protests-what-we-know-about-the-freddie -gray-arrest.

11. Erica L. Green and Kevin Rector, "Students Try to Reclaim Identity," *Baltimore Sun*, April 29, 2015, https://www.baltimoresun.com/maryland/baltimore-city/bs -md-ci-student-protest-message-20150429-story.html.

12. Amy Mulvihill, "Head of the Class: Sonja Santelises Is Ready to Lead Baltimore City Public Schools," *Baltimore*, September 2017, https://www.baltimoremagazine .com/section/educationfamily/sonja-santelises-ready-to-lead-baltimore-city-public -schools/.

13. Erica L. Green, "Baltimore Schools CEO to be Replaced by Former Academics Chief," *Baltimore Sun*, May 3, 2016, https://www.baltimoresun.com/education /bs-md-thornton-out-20160503-story.html.

14. Sonja Santelises (CEO, Baltimore City Public Schools) in discussion with the author, May 2021.

15. The *Blueprint for Success* was launched in the 2017–18 school year and can be found on the Baltimore City Public Schools website, https://www.baltimorecity schools.org/blueprint.

16. Sonja Santelises in discussion with the author, April 2020 and May 2021.

17. Mulvihill, "Head of the Class."

18. Michael Fullan, *Leading in a Culture of Change,* 2nd ed. (San Francisco: Jossey-Bass, 2020).

19. Michelle K. Ryan and S. Alexander Haslam, "The Glass Cliff: Exploring the Dynamics Surrounding the Appointment of Women to Precarious Leadership Positions," *The Academy of Management Review* 32, no. 2 (April 2007): 549–72, doi: 10.5465/AMR.2007.24351856.

20. Michael D. Watkins, *The First 90 Days: Proven Strategies for Getting Up to Speed Faster and Smarter, Updated and Expanded* (Boston: Harvard Business Review Press, 2013).

21. Monica C. Higgins, *Career Imprints: Creating Leaders Across an Industry* (San Francisco: Jossey-Bass, 2005).

22. The Certificate in Advanced Education Leadership (CAEL) is a professional education program at the Harvard Graduate School of Education, chaired by

Elizabeth City. Driving Change is a core component of CAEL designed and taught by Andrés A. Alonso. The framework draws from Jeffrey Pfeffer's work on power in organizations and from Mark Moore's insights into strategic action.

CHAPTER 4

1. All empathy interviews were conducted in confidentiality, and the names of interviewees are withheld.
2. Anthony Bryk and Barbara Schneider, *Trust in Schools: A Core Resource for Improvement*, Rose Series in Sociology (New York: Russell Sage Foundation, 2002).
3. Bryk and Schneider.
4. Bryk and Schneider, 23.
5. Bryk and Schneider, 25.
6. Bryk and Schneider, 24.
7. Bryk and Schneider, 25.
8. Zaretta Hammond (author of *Culturally Responsive Teaching and the Brain* and equity freedom fighter) in discussion with the author, October 2021.
9. Zaretta Hammond, *Culturally Responsive Teaching and the Brain: Promoting Authentic Engagement and Rigor Among Culturally and Linguistically Diverse Students* (Thousand Oaks, CA: Corwin, 2014).
10. Shin Tan (vice principal, East Spring Secondary School, Singapore) in discussion with the author, February 2021.
11. Kim Scott, *Radical Candor: Be a Kick-Ass Boss Without Losing Your Humanity* (New York: St. Martin's Press, 2017), Kindle.
12. Hammond, *Culturally Responsive Teaching and the Brain*; Zaretta Hammond in discussion with the author, October 2021. When working with leaders, the importance of centering proximity in addition to the trust generators cannot be understated. Zaretta Hammond notes that proximity must be prioritized when leading across difference.

CHAPTER 5

1. All empathy interviews were conducted in confidentiality, and the names of interviewees are withheld.
2. Kathryn Pavlovich and Keiko Krahnke, eds., *Organizing Through Empathy* (New York: Routledge, 2014), 1–14.
3. Daniel Goleman, "What Makes a Leader?," *Harvard Business Review*, January 2004, 82–91. We have taken the five components of emotional intelligence described in this article and in Goleman's book *Emotional Intelligence* (New York: Bantam Books, 1995), and explained how it might look when applied to leadership entry.
4. Ann Ishimaru et al., *Recasting Families and Communities as Co-Designers of Education in Tumultuous Times* (Boulder, CO: National Education Policy Center, 2019), http://nepc.colorado.edu/publication/family-leadership.
5. Jason Kamras (superintendent, Richmond Public Schools) in discussion with the author, August 2021.

6. The school district is divided into nine subdistricts, each represented by a member of the school board.
7. Jason Kamras in discussion with the author, August 2021.
8. All empathy interviews were conducted in confidentiality, and the names of interviewees are withheld.
9. Barry C. Jentz and Jerome T. Murphy, "Starting Confused: How Leaders Start When They Don't Know Where to Start," *Phi Delta Kappan* 86, no. 10 (June 2005): 736–44, doi: 10.1177/003172170508601005.
10. "Appreciative Inquiry," Organizing Engagement, https://organizingengagement.org/models/appreciative-inquiry. This website includes a repository of excellent resources on family, youth, and community engagement.
11. "Seven Circle Model," National Equity Project, https://www.nationalequityproject.org/frameworks/seven-circle-model.
12. Adam Waytz, "The Limits of Empathy," *Harvard Business Review*, January–February 2016, 68–73.
13. Safir, *The Listening Leader*, 89.
14. Safir, *The Listening Leader*, 96–97. We reprinted, with permission, the Mindful Listening tool with slight modifications. The original tool can be found in its entirety in the book, and a printable version can be requested on Safir's website, shanesafir.com/resources.

CHAPTER 6

1. Ivory A. Toldson, *No BS (Bad Stats): Black People Need People Who Believe in Black People Enough Not to Believe Every Bad Thing They Hear About Black People* (Boston: Brill Sense, 2019), 3–16, doi: 10.1163/9789004397040.
2. Toldson, 7–9.
3. Toldson, 9–12.
4. Toldson, 12–15.
5. David Herrera (executive director, office of equity, Federal Way Public Schools) in discussion with the author, April 2021.
6. Dr. David Rock and Christine Cox, "SCARF in 2012: Updating the Social Neuroscience of Collaborating with Others," *NeuroLeadership Journal* 4 (2012), https://www.semanticscholar.org/paper/SCARF-®-in-2012%3A-updating-the-social-neuroscience-Cox/ecaa82edd6186fce08b896f17b430e1c9ac7e83b.
7. Robert Kegan, *The Evolving Self: Problem and Process in Human Development* (Cambridge, MA: Harvard University Press, 1982).
8. We want to encourage practitioners to reach out to their organization's research teams for expert support on these analyses, which may require advocating for new ways to look at the data.
9. Nora Gordon and Carrie Conaway, *Common-Sense Evidence: The Education Leader's Guide to Using Data and Research*, Educational Innovations series (Cambridge, MA: Harvard Education Press, 2020), 92–101.
10. Leah Shafer, "When Proficient Isn't Good," *Usable Knowledge,* January 2016, https://www.gse.harvard.edu/news/uk/15/12/when-proficient-isnt-good.

11. Eugene Eubanks, Ralph Parish, and Dianne Smith, "Changing the Discourse in Schools" in *Race, Ethnicity, and Multiculturalism: Policy and Practice,* ed. Peter Hall (New York: Routledge, 1997).

12. Eubanks, Parish, and Smith.

13. "Nature of Discourse(s) in Education—Notes on 'Changing the Discourse in Schools' a.k.a. Discourse I and II 'T' Chart," School Reform Initiative, https://www.schoolreforminitiative.org/download/nature-of-discourses-in-education -notes-on-changing-the-discourse-in-schools-a-k-a-discourse-i-ii-t-chart/.

14. "Nature of Discourse(s) in Education."

15. "The Cynefin Framework," Cynefin Company, https://thecynefin.co/about-us /about-cynefin-framework/.

16. C. F. Kurtz and David J. Snowden, "The New Dynamics of Strategy: Sense-Making in a Complex and Complicated World," *IBM Systems Journal* 42, no. 3 (2003), doi: 10.1147/sj.423.0462; David J. Snowden and Mary E. Boone, "A Leader's Framework for Decision Making," *Harvard Business Review,* November 2007, https://hbr.org/2007/11/a-leaders-framework-for-decision-making.

17. Getting Started with Cynefin (video), Cynefin Company, https://thecynefin.co /about-us/about-cynefin-framework/.

18. In email conversation with David Snowden, November 7, 2021.

CHAPTER 7

1. All empathy interviews were conducted in confidentiality, and the names of interviewees are withheld.

2. Marshall Ganz, "Public Narrative, Collective Action, and Power," in *Accountability Through Public Opinion: From Inertia to Public Action,* ed. Sina Odugbemi and Taeku Lee (Washington, DC: World Bank, 2011), 273–89, http://hdl.handle.net /10986/2296.

3. Ganz, 283–85.

4. Ganz, 285–86.

5. Ganz, 286–88.

6. Kam Gordon (principal, New York City Department of Education) in discussion with the author, May 2021.

7. For further information about the announcing of the Bronx Plan, read Eliza Shapiro, "Bonuses of Up to $8,000 to Teach in Struggling New York Schools," *New York Times,* October 11, 2018, https://www.nytimes.com/2018/10/11/nyregion /nyc-teachers-union-contract.html. If you wish to know more about the process by which new schools were launched as part of the Bronx Plan, read "Mayor de Blasio and Chancellor Carranza Announce 50 Schools to Join Bronx Plan," New York City Office of the Mayor, February 2019, https://www1.nyc.gov/office -of-the-mayor/news/084-19/mayor-de-blasio-chancellor-carranza-50-schools -join-bronx-plan#/0.

8. *I Am* poems are a prompt-based poem structure that allows the author to share details about themselves through biographic phrases, descriptions, and questions.

When completed in groups, the similar structure helps to make connections among people while still lifting up each individual's unique style and identity.

9. Journey line presentations are an artistic biographic practice that allows participants to communicate their personal narrative and the events that led them to the present moment. Typically participants draw a journey on a single sheet of paper with images representing major turning or decision points. They can be narrow and focus on one aspect of a person's identity, such as their career, or they can be broad and discuss an entire life or the life of an organization.

10. Gholdy Muhammad, *Cultivating Genius: An Equity Framework for Culturally and Historically Responsive Literacy* (New York: Scholastic, 2020).

11. Ronald A. Heifetz and Marty Linsky, "When Leadership Spells Danger," *Education Leadership* 61, no. 7 (April 2004): 33–37, https://www.ascd.org/el/articles/when-leadership-spells-danger.

CHAPTER 8

1. Rachel E. Curtis and Elizabeth A. City, *Strategy in Action: How School Systems Can Support Powerful Learning and Teaching* (Cambridge, MA: Harvard Education Press, 2009), 52–56.

2. Stacey Childress, *Note on Strategy in Public Education*, PEL-011 (Cambridge, MA: Public Education Leadership Project at Harvard University, June 2004), https://projects.iq.harvard.edu/files/pelp/files/pel011p2_modified.pdf.

3. Ann M. Ishimaru and Mollie K. Galloway, "Beyond Individual Effectiveness: Conceptualizing Organizational Leadership for Equity," *Leadership and Policy in Schools* 13, no. 1 (2014): 93–146, doi:10.1080/15700763.2014.890733.

4. Ishimaru and Galloway, 101–4.

5. Ishimaru and Galloway, 104–5.

6. Ishimaru and Galloway, 105–6.

7. Jennifer Cheatham (former superintendent of the Madison Metropolitan School District and coauthor of the book) in discussion with her coauthor, September 2021.

8. *Race to Equity: A Baseline Report on the State of Racial Disparities in Dane County* (Madison: Wisconsin Council on Children and Families, 2013), http://racetoequity.net/wp-content/uploads/2016/11/WCCF-R2E-Report.pdf.

9. Wayne Au also uses "canaries in the coal mine" to describe some of the students he knew who were not being served by the system in his chapter "Remembrance: Keeping Kids at the Center of Educational Policy" in William Ayers et al., eds., *City Kids, City Schools: More Reports from the Front Row* (New York: The New Press, 2008), 307.

10. A slightly modified 2015 version of the *Madison Metropolitan School District Strategic Framework* can be found at https://go.boarddocs.com/wi/mmsd/Board.nsf/files/9ZWUQ569A1DD/$file/FrameworkRevised8-27-15c.pdf.

11. The district published an annual report each year from 2013 to 2017, and then a cumulative report after five years in 2018, at the time they decided to pivot their

strategy. This report can be found at https://go.boarddocs.com/wi/mmsd/Board.nsf/files/C6TSQ66B7822/$file/ar5F%20(5).pdf.

12. The "strategic framework engagement process" was laid out in four phases, with regular involvement from the board of education, from October 2017 to August 2018.

13. Jen met with over one thousand people in over fifty meetings during this time frame. In addition to regular meetings with her board, principals, teachers, and members of existing advisory groups, she met with student focus groups (Black, Latinx, Hmong, LGBTQ+, students with disabilities, and opportunity youth), parent focus groups (Black, Latinx, Hmong, parents of ELL students, and parents of students with disabilities), school and central office staff focus groups (staff of color, Black educators, special education assistants, and security assistants) and community member focus groups (youth workers and staff from racial and social justice organizations).

14. Beth Vaade and Amanda Jeppson, *Strategic Framework Engagement—Final Research Report on the Listening and Learning Phase* (Madison, WI: Research and Program Evaluation Office, Madison Metropolitan School District, 2018).

15. The 2018 version of the *Madison Metropolitan School District Strategic Framework* can be found at https://go.boarddocs.com/wi/mmsd/Board.nsf/files/B3744G78E472/$file/Strategic%20Framework%20Final.pdf.

16. Jennifer Cheatham, "Gathering Ideas for MMSD's Strategic Framework," *Madison365*, December 12, 2017, https://madison365.com/gathering-ideas-mmsds-strategic-framework/.

17. Gloria Ladson-Billings, "From the Achievement Gap to the Education Debt: Understanding Achievement in U.S. Schools," *Educational Researcher* 35, no. 7 (October 2006): 3–12, doi: 10.3102/0013189X035007003.

18. John B. Diamond and Jennifer Cheatham, "Ed. Leaders: Discuss Race, Call Out White Supremacy," *Education Week*, April 13, 2021, https://www.edweek.org/leadership/opinion-ed-leaders-be-explicit-about-race-and-white-supremacy/2021/03.

19. Good resources for problem identification and root-cause analysis include: Anthony Bryk et al., *Learning to Improve: How America's Schools Can Get Better at Getting Better* (Cambridge, MA: Harvard Education Press, 2015); James B. Spillane and Amy Franz Coldren, *Diagnosis and Design for School Improvement* (New York: Teachers College Press, 2011); and the National Equity Project's "Seven Circle Model," https://www.nationalequityproject.org/frameworks/seven-circle-model.

20. Ronald Heifetz and Donald L. Laurie, "The Work of Leadership," *Harvard Business Review*, December 2001, https://hbr.org/2001/12/the-work-of-leadership.

CHAPTER 9

1. All empathy interviews were conducted in confidentiality, and the names of interviewees are withheld.

2. Resmaa Menakem, *My Grandmother's Hands: Racialized Trauma and the Pathway to Mending Our Hearts and Bodies* (Las Vegas: Central Recovery Press, 2017), 46.

3. Meghan E. Irons, "I Have Never Seen a Black Superintendent Retire . . . There's a Systemic Problem," *Boston Globe,* July 7, 2021, https://www.bostonglobe.com /2021/07/07/metro/i-have-never-seen-black-superintendent-retire-theres-systemic -problem/; here, Irons describes the challenges that education leaders of color face today.
4. Menakem, *My Grandmother's Hands,* 45.
5. Menakem, *My Grandmother's Hands,* 46.
6. Richard G. Tedeschi, "Growth After Trauma," *Harvard Business Review,* July–August 2020, https://hbr.org/2020/07/growth-after-trauma.
7. Shawn Ginwright, "The Future of Healing: Shifting from Trauma Informed Care to Healing Centered Engagement," *Medium,* May 31, 2018, https://ginwright. medium.com/the-future-of-healing-shifting-from-trauma-informed-care-to -healing-centered-engagement-634f557ce69c.
8. Ginwright, "The Future of Healing."
9. "Restorative Justice and the Circle Process," Healing Justice Project, https://healing justiceproject.org/circle-process.
10. April Warren-Grice, *A Space to Be Whole: A Landscape Analysis of Education-Based Racial Affinity Groups in the U.S.* (Oakland, CA: Black Teacher Project, 2021), https://static1.squarespace.com/static/5c01b0d6b98a78f723592deb/t/60fee8157 02130399ad065fa/1627318296163/BTP+Landscape_Analysis_Racial_Affinity _US_2021.pdf.
11. All empathy interviews were conducted in confidentiality, and the names of interviewees are withheld.
12. We all loved the training we received from Maia Heyck-Merlin, *The Together Leader: Get Organized for Your Success—and Sanity* (San Francisco: Jossey-Bass, 2016), https://www.thetogethergroup.com/books/the-together-leader. These strategies represent just a few of the ideas we picked up that made our work schedules much more manageable.
13. Reba Y. Hodge, "The Year of Scourges: How I Survived Illness and Racism to Find My 'Tribe,'" *Education Week,* April 12, 2021, https://www.edweek.org/leadership /opinion-the-year-of-scourges-how-i-survived-illness-and-racism-to-find-my -tribe/2021/04.

ACKNOWLEDGMENTS

All that could never be said,
All that could never be done,
Wait for us at last
Somewhere back of the sun;

   —SARA TEASDALE, *In the End*

There's no way I can pay you back, but the plan
Is to show you that I understand: You are appreciated

   —TUPAC SHAKUR, *Dear Mama*

First, we are indebted to Barry Jentz, whose mentorship and guidance laid the foundation for our initial leadership moves and for the book. We are honored to build on his good work here.

This book began as a graduate course at the Harvard Graduate School of Education and grew into an online professional learning experience supporting hundreds of leaders internationally. We thank those who contributed to the design of the course, including Carmen Williams and Mitalene Fletcher, because they made the course better. We thank each and every student who "rented these ideas" and helped us all learn along the way. And we thank each of our guest speakers for giving us a view into your work and your authentic leadership.

We have deep gratitude for everyone who trusted us with their stories for this book and the selective vulnerability they demonstrated in sharing them: Kam Gordon, Nancy Gutierrez, David Herrera, Jason Kamras, Sonja Santelises, and Shin Tan. We wish to express our appreciation for everyone who contributed their ideas and feedback: Keith Catone, John Diamond, Zaretta Hammond, Shane Safir, Ivory Toldson, and our friends at the National Equity Project, especially Victor Cary. We also thank every leader who engaged in the empathy interviews that are at the heart of this book.

Our colleague Bonnie Lo made more contributions to this book than we can list. She has been our critical friend, our codesigner, and a ray of sunshine embedding each aspect of the work with positivity, joy, and kindness.

Anne Childers and Arkeelaus "Kee" Sherman graciously offered their artistic talents to help us more deeply understand our approach to leadership entry and to translate our ideas into the graphic representations you see throughout this book.

We have the greatest appreciation for our editorial team at Harvard Education Press: Jayne Fargnoli, Molly Grab, and Nancy Walser. It cannot be easy to work with first-time book authors and these women pushed us and supported us throughout the process.

As we see all work as both personal and professional, each author would like to acknowledge those who have supported us throughout the writing process.

Adam thanks the Mary Gage Peterson and Anne M. Jeans school communities who taught him so much about leadership and what is possible when everyone is committed to realizing the possibilities of each and every student. He thanks his mentors: Deborah Jewell-Sherman, who demonstrates what it means to lead with heart, and David Cohen, who, usually over a cup of tea, encouraged new ways of thinking about the potential of leadership at scale. And his deepest love and gratitude go to his family: Chelsey, Nathan, and Nicky, for constant support throughout this journey.

Rodney thanks his friends and colleagues from the Near North Side, Manierre, Sullivan, and Grambling State University, who continue to provide support, guidance, and friendships that have stood the test of time. Gratitude goes to the many leaders that he's encountered during his professional journey, who modeled what it means to lead with compassion and integrity. To every young person that he has mentored who has overcome unforeseeable obstacles and challenges, who has shown him that if you have someone in your corner who believes in you and sees you for who you are, the sky's the limit. And to his amazing family: Freda, Naphtali, Darrell, Tony, and Shannon, for the unconditional love along the journey.

Jen thanks her colleagues from the Harvard Urban Superintendents Program and Bob Peterkin, who taught her what it means to be an equity-focused leader. She thanks her mentor, Carl Cohn, for teaching her how to lead with humanity. She thanks all of the communities that she has had the privilege to serve, with a special shout-out to the Madison Metropolitan School District, which will always have a special place in her heart. She thanks the many gifted colleagues and dream teams she has had the opportunity to work with, as this work is never something we do alone. And she thanks her family, especially Reg and Theo, "Team Cheatham," for their sweet love and steady support.

Ultimately, we thank you, the readers and leaders, for sharing this moment with us. We hope these words may be useful as you create and sustain communities where each child is loved, and the value of every member is lifted up with purpose and care.

ABOUT THE AUTHORS

JENNIFER PERRY CHEATHAM, EdD, is a senior lecturer at the Harvard Graduate School of Education, cochair of the Ed.M. in Education, Leadership, Organizations, and Entrepreneurship, and cochair of the Public Education Leadership Project. With over twenty-five years of experience in the field of education, she has served as a teacher, teacher leader, professional developer, central office leader, area superintendent, and superintendent. She held leadership roles in the San Diego Unified School District, Chicago Public Schools, and the Madison Metropolitan School District in Wisconsin, where she was superintendent for six and a half years. In each of these roles, she focused on creating instructional coherence, cultivating strong teams, designing systems for professional learning, and strengthening routines for organizational learning to achieve accelerated results for students. During her tenure as superintendent, in partnership with the community she served, she also introduced a new, bolder agenda grounded in a commitment to anti-racism, inclusion, and alliance to children and families of color. She now teaches about system-level leadership at HGSE with a focus on leading for equity, including a course on leadership entry.

RODNEY THOMAS has experience in the education, private, and nonprofit sectors, most recently serving as vice president of national programs at the Surge Institute, where he led the vision and expansion strategy for Surge's fellowship programs. Before that, he was a senior associate at the National Equity Project, where he was responsible for designing and providing unique leadership and organizational development solutions that addressed complex equity-focused change efforts. He began his career as a teacher in the Chicago Public Schools, where he was honored as Teacher of the Year and worked throughout the district leading and supporting several large-scale district initiatives. After spending several years in the classroom, Rodney transitioned into the private sector and worked for companies such as Accenture, Motorola, and Unilever, with a focus on organizational development, executive coaching, and leadership development. His professional journey led him back into the school system working as the special assistant to the superintendent in Madison, Wisconsin, where he supported the superintendent in the implementation of the district's strategic framework. Growing up in the Cabrini-Green neighborhood of Chicago has led him to his life's work. It's his personal "why" that drives the passion he has for supporting underserved communities across the country.

ADAM PARROTT-SHEFFER, EdLD, works with school, district, nonprofit, and business leaders globally to improve learning through data, to design leadership pathways with special attention to entry, and to execute strategy successfully. He teaches university and professional education courses focused on anti-racist coaching, entry for equity leaders, and change management. After teaching middle school literacy and early childhood special education, he spent ten years as an award-winning principal and district administrator—including as a special assistant to the chancellor of the New York City Department of Education where his work focused on increasing access to special education programs and improving academic outcomes for court-involved youth. He used all these experiences to support thousands of educators as a senior leader with the New

Teacher Center, where Adam coached principal supervisors and superintendents and led impact strategy. Adam champions joyful learning, youth agency, and collaborative change as a board member of Playworks Illinois and Harvard's Data Wise Project. His most meaningful work in education is serving as a volunteer at the neighborhood school in Chicago that his children attend.

INDEX